Teaching Notes

on Piano Exam Pieces

2019 & 2020

Grades 1-8

Andrew Eales

Fiona Lau

Murray McLachlan

Frances Wilson

ABRSM

First published in 2018 by ABRSM (Publishing) Ltd, a wholly owned
subsidiary of ABRSM, 4 London Wall Place, London EC2Y 5AU,
United Kingdom

Reprinted in 2018

ISBN 978 1 78601 075 9
AB 3933

Cover by Kate Benjamin & Andy Potts, with thanks to Brighton College
Printed in England by Halstan & Co. Ltd, Amersham, Bucks., on materials
from sustainable sources

CONTENTS

FOREWORD

by ABRSM Chief Examiner, John Holmes

Choosing new pieces is always exciting – rather like setting out on a journey to somewhere you haven't been before. As a teacher, you are presented with an opportunity to match your students' skills and preferences to the right music for them, while also making use of your expertise to ensure the right level of challenge to encourage the development of technique and musicianship. This book is intended to help guide you in making good decisions, together with your student, about which pieces will work most successfully. It sets out to provide useful insights into each piece, which we hope will support you and your students on your teaching and learning journeys.

The expert contributors are all piano teachers with a wealth of experience. They are able to draw from their knowledge and understanding to provide valuable hints and tips, as well as helpful advice on how to develop the musical relationship that links composer, score and performer.

In fact, the choice of piece is only the first in an almost never-ending series of choices which becomes the learning journey I mentioned at the beginning. Whether it's Cimarosa, Chopin or Clementi, Skryabin, Shostakovich or Schumann, a whole range of decisions – conscious and subconscious – will need to be made in order for the developing pianist to arrive at their destination, in this case, the exam performance. Tempo, touch, fingering, pedalling, phrasing ... the list of choices goes on, so perhaps it would be helpful here to talk about how the decision-making process might be approached.

It is crucial to note that there is no 'ABRSM way' of playing any of our piano exam pieces, although of course there *is* an 'ABRSM way' of assessing how they are played. This is by considering the overall musical outcome – in effect, the cumulative result of all the various musical and technical decisions that will have been made in preparing the performance. For example, ABRSM examiners don't assess fingering, but we do comment on and evaluate its effects, such as evenness of tone or regularity of delivery, which are so often partly the result of fingering choices. Examiners are listening and looking for the degree of skill a candidate shows in controlling elements of pitch, time, tone, shape and performance, which develop gradually during their learning and practice prior to the exam. It is these elements that form the basis of our marking criteria, which are used by examiners in all ABRSM practical graded exams.

Between them, the ABRSM scores, recordings and *Teaching Notes* are intended to open a variety of doorways to interpretation. There may well be differences between what the scores imply, what the recordings present and what these *Teaching Notes* recommend – but in reality they do not so much contradict as complement each other. We would like to encourage you to inspire your students to play with creativity and individuality, leading them to achieve successful performances that suit and reflect their particular skills, strengths and enthusiasms.

That's the excitement of every musical journey – there will always be a variety of routes to a successful musical result, and our examiners do not mark candidates according to any particular one; instead they judge the combined effectiveness of the various musical performance decisions you and your student have made, taken as a whole. This means that every candidate can play to their strengths, not only in their particular choice of pieces, but also in the way that they interpret them. For example, there is a range of tempos – a 'bandwidth' of speeds – at which any given piece can successfully be played. For some pieces this will be wider than for others, but even where a metronome mark is given, there is usually room for some flexibility of approach. The examiner will not be marking the speed of playing absolutely or in isolation, but rather in conjunction with other elements of performance, such as note accuracy and rhythmic character. The right tempo choice for each student is best determined as part of a comfortable balance between the speed and other elements, so that one thing is not sacrificed to another – precision sacrificed to speed, for example.

Other decisions to be made include phrasing, ornament realization, whether to add dynamics, play straight or swing quavers, and when to use the pedal. The examiner will be assessing the overall musical outcome, rather than the strict observance of any printed pedal indications, which means that these may be adapted or omitted to suit the needs of the individual. However, it is important to bear in mind the strengths of your student. Therefore, pieces whose full musical effect is heavily reliant on pedalling (whether marked in the music or not) might best be avoided if appropriate pedalling cannot be managed.

It is worth reiterating that using the ABRSM marking criteria (which can be found online and within the Piano syllabus), examiners will assess the musical outcome heard on the day: the musical effectiveness of the piano playing in the exam room. The best results will arise from a well-judged match between each individual candidate's piano skills, and the particular demands of the chosen piece.

Candidates can choose the order in which they play their three pieces, and whether to start the exam with these or another section – scales, for example. Once again there is no single right way; as with so much of the musical learning journey leading to performance, the exam itself starts with a decision!

We do hope that you will feel excited and inspired by the wonderful range of musical possibilities open to you and your students within the 2019 & 2020 ABRSM Piano syllabus. Spanning around 400 years of composition, whether it's Kuhlau or Khachaturian, there is truly something for everyone to embark upon and enjoy.

ABOUT THE AUTHORS

All of the authors have a wealth of teaching experience, which covers a wide variety of musical styles. Each author has contributed to a mixture of grades and lists. The initials shown above each teaching note can be used to identify its author.

ANDREW EALES (AE)

Andrew is a pianist, teacher and writer. He graduated from the University of Birmingham, subsequently studying at the Royal College of Music, where he specialized in authentic performance practice. Andrew spent several years as Head of Keyboard for the Milton Keynes Music Service, during which time his *Keyquest* series of electronic keyboard tutor books was published. He is in demand as an educational consultant and mentor and his original compositions have appeared in several publications, including the *Mosaic* series (Editions Musica Ferrum) and ABRSM's *Keyboards Together* and *Piano Star* series.

FIONA LAU (FL)

Fiona has a Master's degree in Psychology for Musicians and many years' experience of piano teaching at all levels and ages. She is now a consultant, advising on general instrumental teaching, grade exam preparation and diploma training. She has delivered presentations for the publisher Hal Leonard and mentored for the University of Sheffield music department and Essex Music Service. Fiona is a regular reviewer for *Music Teacher* magazine and has also edited and arranged the educational piano books *Songs of Great Britain and Ireland* and *Treasured Classics*, published by Fentone Music.

MURRAY MCLACHLAN

Murray is Head of Keyboard at Chetham's School of Music, a senior tutor at the Royal Northern College of Music and Chair of the European Piano Teachers' Association UK. As a pianist he has made over 40 commercial recordings. Murray is the founder and Artistic Director of Chetham's International Summer School and Festival for Pianists, and the Manchester International Concerto Competition for Young Pianists. As a writer he has contributed to *International Piano* and *BBC Music Magazine*. His books *The Foundations of Technique, Piano Technique in Practice* and *The Psychology of Piano Technique* are published by Faber Music.

FRANCES WILSON

Frances is a pianist, teacher, concert reviewer, writer and blogger on classical music and pianism. She is a regular writer for classical music websites InterludeHK and IDAGIO, and has contributed many articles on aspects of piano playing to *Pianist* magazine's online content, as well as a series of essays on Schubert's penultimate piano sonata for *The Schubertian*, the journal of the Schubert Institute (UK). She has also appeared on BBC Radio 3's *Music Matters* to discuss the role of music criticism today and the effect of the internet on music journalism.

HOW TO USE THIS BOOK

In *Teaching Notes*, every note contains teaching ideas relating to three areas of learning: musical context, technical challenges, and performance and interpretation.

Syllabus list numbers and author initials are shown at the top of each piece, either side of the composer name and piece title, for example:

A:1 **Attwood** Theme

 MUSICAL CONTEXT

The first section explains where the piece fits within the world of music, and introduces the distinctive features of the piece. Genre, period, structure and style may be mentioned here, as well as information about the composer. You might also find suggestions of music to listen to, which will help your student gain familiarity with the musical context.

TECHNICAL CHALLENGES

In this section the trickiest corners of the piece are identified and suggestions to help tackle them are provided. Alternative ornament realizations and fingering may appear here, as well as practice ideas to help with agility and coordination.

PERFORMANCE AND INTERPRETATION

This section focuses on communicating the music with style and personality. These elements can help turn an accurate performance into one with real artistic value.

General advice about interpreting the score, hand stretch, pedalling and repeats can be found in the Piano syllabus, under 'Piano requirements and information'.

GRADE 1

A:1 **Attwood** Theme (FL)

The attractive flow of the RH melody of this Theme appears to owe much to Attwood's years as a chorister in the Chapel Royal and to his time studying with Mozart. The underlying Alberti bass supports the melody and gives harmonic interest. Students will be delighted to note that in a clear ABA structure the opening eight bars are repeated to form the final section.

Legato and gentle staccato warm-up scales in D major will help bring familiarity with the key and the articulation needed for this piece. The LH Alberti bass may be learnt by recognizing the different chord patterns in each section and playing them as solid chords. Each section may then be played as a duet with teacher and student taking one hand apiece, first with solid chords in the LH and then as written. The shift of hand position at bar 5 will need attention in order to be managed without disrupting the flow, and the RH fingering from 1 to 4 in bar 6 is another element to isolate in practice. In the B section keeping fingers close to the keys may help achieve a controlled *p*.

The most sophisticated performances will have the RH melody singing out against a quieter LH. Marking in a softer dynamic for the LH on the score may help here, but an appropriate balance and effective dynamics overall will be achieved through careful listening.

A:2 **Duncombe** Minuet in C (FL)

Duncombe's pieces are often found in pedagogical collections, and rightly so; they are attractive and relatively straightforward to play. This piece is sometimes known as the 'Fanfare Minuet' as the opening *f* four bars demand the listener's attention. The excitement increases with the RH's repeated notes, two- and three-note chords and the sustained *f* passages.

To keep the tempo steady it is important to adhere to a suitable fingering, whether playing what is printed or making different choices. The more unexpected fingerings given (e.g. RH finger 2 in bar 3) need extra practice to achieve a smooth melodic flow. The LH supports the RH so practising first LH, then RH, before LH again may help to secure dynamics and the open-hand arpeggios. A good hand posture throughout, with curved fingers, and ensuring that the RH fifth finger does not collapse in bars 10–16, should enable a strong, even tone. At cadences, isolating the RH jump from finger 3 to a chord for repeated practice before adding the LH will increase security. Care should be taken to articulate the marked slurs correctly.

Extra light and shade given to the dynamics could add further interest. Starting *mf*, for example, and making a crescendo towards *f* at the minim C in bar 4 would build excitement. A stylish finish might include a very slight rallentando in the final two bars, as if to bow and curtsey, with hands coming off gracefully at the end.

A:3 **Anon. 15th-century English** Agincourt Song   FL

Folksongs such as this act as time capsules and so 600 years later we can recreate the joy of victory at Agincourt by singing and playing this rousing 'carol'. Many performances of the song, which also featured in the film *Henry V* starring Laurence Olivier, can be found on YouTube. It is written as a strophe (verse) and burden (chorus) and would originally have comprised many more verses giving details of the battle.

Although the RH (representing the singer) has the tune, the LH has some independence and individual articulation. It is nearly all in a five-finger hand position, with the exception of finger 2 on the B♭ in bar 10 and the stretch down to C in bar 11. Singing, clapping and then playing the RH may help to embed it thoroughly. Both parts will be secured by separate-hands practice and by teacher and student playing a hand each. Tapping RH and LH together is a useful intermediate step before attempting to play the piece slowly hands together, and in four-bar sections.

The most effective performances will include all the articulation and dynamic changes and manage a quick tempo with a triumphant slowing-down at the end of the *ff* Deo gratias. However, the tempo choice needs to bear in mind that a musical performance will be one in which articulation and dynamics are not sacrificed for the sake of speed.

A:4 **W. F. Bach** Air in A minor   FL

W. F. Bach, the eldest of J. S. Bach's sons, is often known as the 'Halle Bach' on account of his years spent there. This delicate little dance-like melody has elements of his father's polyphony combined with the expressive 'Empfindsamkeit' style.

The two-part nature of this piece suggests opportunities for separate-hands practice, and teacher and student might play it as a duet, taking one hand apiece. There are a number of places, particularly in the LH, where the fingering requires deft repositioning of the hand; these will benefit from isolation and repeated practice. The RH legato phrases may be better understood and made secure if they are sung – with a breath at the end of each phrase, and noting where a phrase flows over the bar-line. Words might also be made up to fit the rhythms. Warm-up scales and broken chords in A minor will familiarize students with the key.

In the most sophisticated performances the LH will remain legato throughout, against the RH phrasing; however, an alternative might be a LH articulation that follows the RH phrase marks. The crescendo marked at bar 8b suggests a warmer *mf* for the middle section before the *p* of the last four bars. A gentle rallentando in the last two bars might provide a stylish courtly bow in keeping with the dance-like style.

A:5 **Haydn** Quadrille   (FL)

Haydn composed many dances for orchestra or military band, with several subsequently transcribed for keyboard. A quadrille was a square dance for four couples, popular in Europe in the late-eighteenth and nineteenth centuries. In this example the RH has a jaunty little melody dancing on top of a LH consisting of only two chords.

Ensuring that fingers are firm and pressed down together will prevent the chords from sounding too heavy. Practising first on the piano lid and then transferring these *stacc. sempre* chords to the keys and listening carefully for a clear, even sound will help to produce a suitable tone. Playing the chords *p* with a metronome could aid steadiness, and create a good balance between melody and accompaniment. Clapping the RH can secure the rhythms against the pulse, particularly the pairs of quavers, while singing it may help to establish its articulation and the different note values.

A sophisticated performance will have staccato crotchets that are not too short and percussive and a quieter final LH note at each cadence. Allegretto is not as quick a speed as Allegro but, when choosing a tempo, students should remember that the music is still to sound dance-like. This quadrille was not composed for a modern piano so a warm rather than a harsh *f* will be true to the courtly image and give a more authentic feel to the performance.

A:6 **Türk** A Lovely Day   (FL)

This keyboard piece from Türk's impressive teaching output has an elegant RH melody supported by a gentle LH. It is typical of the Classical era, and has a clearly demarcated structure which students should be encouraged to recognize – particularly the B section with its change of material and dynamic.

The B section has a clearly marked dynamic progression from *p* to *mp* to *mf*. Encouraging students to lift their hands slightly off the keys at the end of each phrase and consider how to place them down again to achieve the dynamic will help the progression to be heard. In several places one hand is legato and the other staccato. One way to secure this is to tap out these short passages on the piano lid, holding down the legato hand and making the staccato notes lifted and short. Students must take care over the diminuendo in the RH of bar 4 as the LH gets louder, and should enjoy the graceful *poco rit.* and diminuendo at the end.

In effective performances there will be a good balance between the RH's cantabile melody and the accompanying LH. The staccato notes are marked to be played *portato*, which means a semi-staccato rather than anything more percussive, and practising them legato, staccato and then *portato* should elicit the desired effect. Discussing what is happening on this 'Lovely Day' might help to bring the piece alive.

B:1 **Brahms** Wiegenlied (Cradle Song) (FW)

This beautiful lullaby or 'cradle song' by Brahms is one of his most popular and best-known works and the charming simplified version here gives early pianists a wonderful introduction to his music. It was originally for voice and piano, and this arrangement for solo piano presents the gentle, soothing melody over a simple rocking accompaniment in the LH.

Each phrase of the melody lies comfortably under the hand. The octave stretches in bars 8–9 and 12–13 can be managed if students, particularly those with smaller hands, allow their hand to be guided by the movement of the wrist rather than attempting to stretch the full octave. The LH accompaniment should be soft and gentle, with slightly more emphasis on the first note of each two-note slur. In bars 9–10 and 13–14 the LH may be brought out a little more. There are ample opportunities to explore the individual 'character' of intervals and to experiment with dynamics to highlight these. A tiny pause, or agogic accent, between the lower and upper Cs in bars 8–9 will add more emotion to this particular interval and reflect how it would be approached by a singer.

As befits a cradle song, designed to rock a baby to sleep, the atmosphere of the music should be gentle and soothing. A sweetly singing sound in the RH melody within a restrained dynamic range will be effective.

B:2 **Oesten** The Echo

Marked Pastorale, meaning a style of music that evokes the countryside, this piece suggests the echoes of a hunting horn or perhaps a yodeller in the mountains. It is a cheerful miniature which offers the opportunity to explore contrasting dynamics and registers, creating a characterful narrative within only 18 bars of music.

The LH is very simple, comprising just four different chords which underpin the repeated motifs in the RH melody. The 'echoes' are created by shifting the RH position up an octave and each one is marked ***pp***. To accurately manage the move between different positions on the keyboard, students should practise moving as quickly as possible from the lower note and waiting over the upper note, only playing it when certain that their finger is over the correct note. A firm pulse will keep the music rhythmic with a good sense of forward movement. The triplet groups may be practised by clapping the rhythm before playing them.

As the 'echoes' are in the upper register of the piano, it should be easy to control the sound. The aim should be for a bright f and a delicate, distant pp for real contrast. Accents provide greater emphasis and contrast and add to the upbeat mood of the music.

B:3 Swinstead The Lonely Road

The minor key and modal character of this piece, with its simple, rather melancholy melody, suggest a lonely walk along an unknown path. English pianist and composer Felix Swinstead wrote primarily for the piano and many of his works have found their way into the repertoire of young pianists.

The melody, taken by the RH, lies comfortably under the fingers with no awkward jumps or stretches. This will provide the opportunity to explore legato playing: students should be encouraged to maintain close contact with the keys and to move smoothly between each note. In bars 8 and 11 the LH phrases can be given more prominence to add contrast. Each phrase needs to be clearly delineated with a fractional gap to signify the end of one phrase and the beginning of a new one. Good independence of fingers in the LH is helpful in bars 3, 9 and 16 to ensure that the lower note is sustained while the upper notes move.

The subdued mood of this piece is reflected in its restrained dynamic palette, but some contouring of the phrases (a little crescendo and diminuendo within each phrase) will add colour and interest. The simple LH accompaniment should be balanced against the RH melody. A fragment of the main melody returns for the coda in bars 17–18 and is marked *rall.*, bringing the music to a quiet close.

B:4 Bartók Quasi adagio

This piece comes from the first volume of Bartók's *For Children*, a suite of piano pieces of increasing difficulty aimed at young piano students and based on Hungarian folk tunes. Its haunting melody and slow, dance-like rhythms should appeal to both children and adults, and will suit students with a good sense of rhythm and pulse and well-developed tone control.

The RH melody lies very comfortably under the hand in a five-finger position and is an excellent introduction to the 'drop slur' technique. Students should be encouraged to drop the wrist a little below the keyboard on the first note of the slur and 'float' up and off the second note. This will also enhance the rhythmic details. In the LH chords, observing the suggested fingering and articulating the wrist and hand into the second chord will ensure a smooth transition. Students should watch out for the change in the organization of the LH chords from bar 11, and especially in bars 16–18.

 An effective performance will be rhythmical with a well-shaped melody that is sensitively balanced against the LH chords, and will have a feel for the rather serious yet poignant character of the piece. Both melody and LH chords should follow the dynamic markings to give contour and expression to each phrase.

B:5   **Andrew Eales** Head in the Clouds   (FW)

This attractive and accessible piece by the British teacher, pianist and composer Andrew Eales will appeal to students of all ages. A lilting melody, with a simple two-note accompaniment, is played first in the RH and then in the LH, an octave lower.

The scalic melody lies easily under the hand in a comfortable five-finger position, facilitating a smooth legato. The accompaniment comprises tied notes with rising intervals, offering teacher and student the opportunity to explore the characteristics and expressive qualities of different intervals. Both melody and accompaniment can be practised in unison which will help with note security.

Despite its simplicity, this piece has a thoughtful, rather melancholy mood and offers plenty of scope for expressive playing. The dynamics should be shaped according to the contours of each phrase and the focus of practice will be to bring out the melody, especially when it moves to the LH. Good attention should be paid to the rest in bar 18 and to the change of tempo and subsequent pause in bars 19–20, as these elements really enhance the music's character. The final bar may be pedalled, the foot lifting slowly off the pedal to allow the sound – as indicated by the composer – to 'die away to nothing'.

B:6   **Andrew Lloyd Webber** Close every door

This is the big solo number from the hugely popular musical *Joseph and the Amazing Technicolor Dreamcoat*, and although this is a simplified version, it still packs quite a punch in its emotional and lyrical qualities. Students who know or have seen the musical will especially enjoy the opportunity to play this attractive, expressive piece.

The LH part is straightforward, and provides the harmonic foundations over which the RH melody soars. Both parts lie comfortably under the hand, though a change of position is required in the RH at bars 9–10. Although it is not necessary to play the repeat in the exam, some explanation of first- and second-time bars will help students understand how the repeats work.

 Marked Andante espressivo, the music should move forward without dragging – with smooth legato phrases and well-sustained LH notes. Although not marked explicitly, some crescendo and diminuendo within each phrase will add extra shape and feeling, and listening to a recording of the original song will offer further ideas about expression. Bars 10–13 should have a distinctly different dynamic level; the mood is more hopeful here, if only briefly, before the tragic character of the opening returns. A slight ritardando in the final two bars will bring the music to a hushed, understated close.

C:1 Ian King Happy Day (AE)

This good-natured piece is the work of Ian King, a pianist, teacher and composer whose music encompasses a varied range of genres. Here he writes in a popular swing style, and this piece is a great introduction to the world of jazz piano.

Although this piece includes no awkward stretches, it does require regular changes of hand position. Practising the jump with the RH thumb from G to E (as in bars 6–7 and 13–14), observing the arm movement involved and working on precision, may help students develop confidence. This jump helps with clear phrasing, but the rest of the piece will benefit from a similar attention to phrase ends and note groupings. The final RH chords will also need some careful work, and some players may prefer fingers 4 and 2 for the very last chord.

Those who haven't played swing quavers before may need help to learn the timing aurally, using teacher demonstrations or a recording of the piece. 'Call and response' clapping games can also really help. Meanwhile, the LH needs particular clarity. The rests in the LH (bars 9–14) should be contrasted with the held minims elsewhere. Dynamic variety – and particularly the drop to *p* in bars 9–12 – will add much to a performance, which will also gain from not being too heavy-handed!

C:2 J. M. Last Who Said Mice?

This amusing piece comes from Joan Last's imaginative 1964 collection entitled *Cats*, in which each of the ten short pieces ingeniously presents aspects of the feline character. 'Who Said Mice?' conveys the alertness of the predator, and the piece's astute portrayal is sure to delight all cat lovers!

The music encompasses a wide range of notes, with each hand using both treble and bass clef. Students will need to read the leger-line notes carefully, and be ready to cross hands where required; the LH in bars 4 and 12 can be a particular surprise. The unison quavers here need to be well managed, with hands properly together. The two-note slurs which appear in each hand can be practised in isolation, noting the fall and rise of the wrist in each couplet. Particular focus will be needed to retain a sense of pulse in the final line, which presents an unusual and potentially challenging combination of *dim. molto, più mosso*, and notes descending to the lowest register, ***pp***.

Last was a highly influential teacher who placed great importance on what she called 'freedom technique', so it is no wonder that the pieces from *Cats* all highlight important pedagogic issues. In this case, gradation of tone and dynamic are crucial. Staccato notes need to be crisp but light, and the image of a cat's floppy paw is a most potent one for conveying the soft wrist needed for success.

`C:3` **Kevin Wooding** The Egyptian Level

Pauline Hall's hugely popular *Piano Time* series has spawned many enjoyable repertoire collections, and *Spooky Piano Time* (from which this piece is taken) is a particular favourite. 'The Egyptian Level' is a vivid piece, its evocative Arabic scale patterns stimulating the imagination, while also providing teachers and students with an opportunity to discuss the important role of scale and key.

This piece includes very high and low treble-clef notes, and care is needed reading the leger lines. Although it will be tempting to write in some letter names, it is a better idea to try to memorize the notes and where they come on the piano for fluent recall. The frequent augmented 2nds in the RH will feel unfamiliar, and it can help to hold down the keys for all the notes in each five-finger position, directing attention on how each stretch feels under the hand.

Balance between the hands is essential so that the tune remains in focus. The LH needs control, avoiding any harshness of tone; maintaining flexible wrists will aid the staccato 5ths, avoiding excess arm movement. The composer emphasizes the importance of a legato RH tone, and some arm weight will be needed here. Students might exaggerate the tempo changes in the final line, making sure that the 'a tempo' in bar 13 matches the opening. A wonderful effect can be created by the ***pp*** ending – the final RH notes disappearing in a wisp of pedal.

`C:4` **Heather Hammond** In the Scrum

The 15 books in Heather Hammond's *Cool Piano* series have proved highly popular, each including a collection of imaginative pieces. 'In the Scrum' is one of the more rock-influenced pieces from the second volume of *Cool Piano Sport*. Students with an electronic keyboard can practise this (as with all the pieces in the book) with a backing beat and the instrument voicing suggested, before trying to convey the musical feel at a piano.

The RH uses notes in 3rds, going as low as the F below middle C; accurate reading of leger lines is important. Care should be taken to play staccato notes as written, and holding the tied notes for their full length emphasizes the syncopated rhythm stylishly. To help establish a good staccato feel for the LH repeated notes, students might practise the first two bars (and similar) using a fingering of 1-2-3-4-5-4-3-2. After reverting to the easy fingering in the score, a soft wrist movement will help to regulate touch and prevent tension.

Dynamics play an important part in the narrative of this piece, conveying the rising tension 'in the scrum'. Starting as quietly as possible will allow for an exciting crescendo throughout the piece. The steep diminuendo from f to p in the final two bars – with no rallentando – brings the music to an effective close.

C:5 **John Kember** Gospel Song (AE)

John Kember's wide-ranging career has taken him from music teaching to success as a composer, arranger, pianist, conductor and recording artist. Kember's *16 Pieces for Piano Solo*, from which this charming 'Gospel Song' comes, is a collection of jazz-inspired pieces which provide an enjoyable introduction to a wide range of popular music idioms.

Establishing a strong sense of the pulse is essential from the start, and students may find it helpful to play along with a metronome or keyboard drum beat. Rests must be counted carefully, especially where they appear on the downbeat. The RH requires quick position changes; in bar 1 (and similar) the D should be held as long as possible before the move to the chord in bar 2. Many of the chords are marked *mp* and care must be taken to ensure their notes are played together, and with an even voicing.

This piece can be considered a gentle introduction to swing, and playing it in swing time is highly effective. But the piece should be perfected with straight quavers for the exam, while keeping the cool gospel feel. This is helped by close attention to dynamics and articulation. The staccato cadence resolutions throughout should be played lightly. Students might also enjoy trying the original, chordal ending, although the easier alternative is required for the exam.

C:6 **S. Wilson** The Witch (AE)

This frightening character piece comes from Stanley Wilson's picturesque collection of 16 easy pieces telling the familiar tale of Hansel and Gretel.

Students who love the story and enjoy 'The Witch' will no doubt wish to explore the whole collection!

This piece uses a wide note range, and players must familiarize themselves with leger-line notes in both clefs. Before your student begins learning the piece it would be advisable to point out that from bar 25 both hands are in the bass clef. 'The Witch' also affords an opportunity to consider new and unusual intervals, some of which require stretches. Smaller hands might prefer fingers 2-5-1 in bar 14, and this can be repeated in bars 18–19. Articulation plays a large part in establishing the overall mood. Accents on the third beat of bars 4–6 create an element of shock, and can be played heavily. The softer staccato RH from the last beat of bar 7 allows the LH tune to stand out; care must be taken to ensure the LH doesn't play detached at the same time.

With its imaginative title and wide dynamic range, 'The Witch' invites an expressive response. The character marking – 'Ugly and forbidding' – allows scope for trying different tempos, while perhaps encouraging a pace that is moderate rather than overly quick. The **pp** ending is another challenge – a soft staccato rather than a physical bounce will deliver a more sinister conclusion.

GRADE 2

A:1   **Diabelli**   Lesson in C   (AE)

This elegant Allegretto by the Austrian composer Anton Diabelli is a model of Viennese Classical charm and melodic poise. Looking at paintings from the time, and photos of Vienna itself, might help to fire the imagination – but equally it could prove helpful and interesting for students to listen to a performance, either by their teacher or from a recording, and consider what the music brings to mind.

Tidy fingerwork is essential in this piece. The RH semiquavers could easily become uneven, and may benefit from practice using alternate dotted rhythms. Some of the stretches in the LH may prove awkward for smaller hands, especially because of the moving hand position, so will need extra care. Also, it is necessary to be alert to the balance between the hands, especially in bars 17–24, where a different articulation is required in each. In this passage the LH may be prone to tension, which will militate against even playing, so suppleness is needed here, and some slight rotation of the wrist.

The indicated tempo, combined with the crisp articulation and accents, ensures that a chirpy mood is established. Paying attention to the generous amount of dynamics and phrasing given (some of it editorial) will help convey the shape of each phrase. Equally important is to try to communicate the overall dynamic shape and contrasts, which will add significantly to the performance.

A:2   **Anon.**   Musette in D   (AE)

The famous Notebook for Anna Magdalena Bach of 1725 remains a compilation of wonderful and varied Baroque pieces, many of which are as educative as they are excellent. This popular and lively Musette is thought to be by one of J. S. Bach's sons. With its rustic vigour and bouncing LH patterns, this piece has long been a firm favourite with students and audiences alike.

The jumping hand positions may pose a challenge, and the tempo chosen should be one that allows time for the hands to switch octave repeatedly and accurately throughout. Playing the opening LH octave with the RH notes as a closed D major triad, then moving quickly to the triad positions of bar 3, and back again, will help students learn and remember the distance of travel. Bars 13–16 may also be challenging, especially for smaller hands, and will gain from careful slow practice, keeping a supple wrist when moving between RH positions.

Including dynamic light and shade will prevent a performance from becoming tiring for the listener, and the middle section offers the perfect spot for some quieter playing, as the editorial *p* indicates. With the second section being longer than the first, the final da capo is short, so to achieve an effective conclusion to the piece, a ritenuto might be included in the final two bars.

A:3 **Telemann** Gigue à l'Angloise (Gigue in the English Style) (AE)

The jig was popular in England from the sixteenth century, but by Telemann's time it was usually a more complex, contrapuntal piece. This *Gigue à l'Angloise* offers a simpler approach, with clear four-bar phrases and the lively duple time of the earlier dance. It comes from *Der getreue Music-Meister* (The True Music Master), a publication that enabled ordinary people to experience music that had formerly been the preserve of the wealthy. Telemann focused on providing pieces for amateur domestic music-making, and hoped to offer a complete overview of musical styles.

Perhaps as in the dance itself, the challenge here lies in navigating the numerous large jumps, especially in the LH. They require carefully worked-out fingering, positioning the hands optimally for each leap. The pairs of notes in each jump may be tried in isolation, starting slowly and accelerating to full speed and beyond. Another helpful trick is to play all the notes as dotted-crotchet chords, learning their shapes and internalizing the harmony.

Adapting harpsichord pieces for the modern piano is always an interesting musical challenge. The key to success is often developing effective articulation. Playing with less speed, but with crisp delivery, adds energy to a performance. The dynamics and articulation given in the score are editorial; though effective for a stylish performance they are not prescriptive, so students can feel free to try alternatives!

A:4 **Clementi** Arietta in F (AE)

This charming Arietta, which perfectly captures Clementi's lyrical melodic style, comes from his *An Introduction to the Art of Playing on the Pianoforte*. Published in 1801, this quickly became the bestselling tutor of its day, and is known to have been the choice of Beethoven and Chopin in their teaching.

Clear phrasing is essential throughout, and the RH rest in bar 6 allows for the hand to move position while offering a good opportunity to discuss the ends of phrases. Similar phrasing can be applied in bars 2, 8 and 10. The ornaments in bars 3 and 11 are appoggiaturas. These share the value of the main note, so should be played as equal semiquavers on the beat. The held LH notes at the start provide a challenge, but help to define the unhurried allegretto pace. Encourage students to work on the LH separately. Bar 8 requires particular care, but Clementi's fingering supports the return of the main tune.

Note should be taken of the ¢ time signature when setting a tempo, and students should be encouraged to gently emphasize this pulse, but without rushing. The key to a good performance of this piece is a well-phrased cantabile RH, with effective balance between the hands. In practice, benefits can be gained from exaggerating the phrasing, and from exploring the role that a flexible wrist can play.

A:5 **Handel** Air (Hornpipe) in D minor (AE)

Dating from 1717/18, the Air (Hornpipe) in D minor, HWV 461, belongs to the varied assortment of short pieces composed by Handel for the harpsichord around that time. The title 'Air (Hornpipe)' suggests that the piece combines the song-like qualities of the air with the more buoyant rhythm of the hornpipe, a popular dance in England in Handel's day which was similar to the jig but in simple rather than compound time.

Both RH and LH move across a wide range of the keyboard in this piece; happily, the suggested fingering works very well, if it is followed carefully. An even balance between the hands should be sought, highlighting the interest of the moving bass line. The unusual beaming in the notation (e.g. in the RH at bar 8) is faithful to the original. Although this initially may appear confusing, spotting the three beats of the bar and counting carefully should ensure that the rhythms soon fall into place.

A tempo that is firmly based in three- rather than one-in-a-bar works well for this piece, and a medium *mf* dynamic can be maintained throughout. Emphasizing the rise and fall of each phrase adds expressive weight to the performance, as will lightly accenting the syncopated notes in the RH. To assist with clarity, the LH can be played non-legato, while the RH tune remains legato, cantabile.

A:6 **Haydn** Allegro (AE)

Joseph Haydn's Sonata (or Divertimento) in G, Hob. XVI:8, is a short work in four movements, of which this is the joyful finale. It is thought to have been composed in 1766, originally for harpsichord. The jaunty melody and showy semiquavers have helped establish the movement as a favourite with students, and the piece is excellent for the development of finger independence and dexterity.

The semiquavers here need to be kept even, and not too hurried. Played legato, they highlight the simple chord structure, which you might wish to discuss with students. Small hands might play just the lower notes of the octave bass line in bars 13–16, giving them extra emphasis. The suggested fingering in the RH in bar 14 could be altered to use finger 2 on A, but if so fingers 4 and 5 will need to play evenly in bar 15.

The $\frac{3}{8}$ time signature can be emphasized with a slight tenuto on the first quaver in each bar and lightly articulated second and third quavers in the melody line only, adding a sense of bounce. This can be copied in the LH in bars 9–16, while noting the held bass notes in bars 9–11. The (editorial) dynamics nicely emphasize the character of the music, and are stylistically suitable for a modern instrument, but students can be encouraged to experiment with, and evaluate, alternatives.

B:1 **Burgmüller** Arabesque (FL)

Burgmüller's Arabesque has featured many times on exam syllabuses and is a favourite in student concerts and competitions. It will suit those who enjoy the drama of rapid RH five-finger patterns against crisp, clean LH chords.

A useful way to begin is to practise the RH and LH patterns in isolation, listening for an even tone and a staccato lift at the end. The hand shifts should then be worked at until they are in time and secure. Using dotted rhythms and then staccato for the semiquaver runs in practice will improve finger strength and independence. The more lyrical section B calls for good hand independence, which will entail slow separate-hands practice followed by hands played together, still slowly; only then should the tempo be increased. The end of the piece will benefit from practice looking at the music, looking at the hands, with eyes open and eyes closed. Independent learning can be encouraged by having students record and listen to their performance for accuracy and a characterful interpretation of the score.

An effective performance will have a consistent tempo, and lots of separate-hands as well as metronome practice will help achieve this. There should be clear *p* and *f* contrasts, thrilling crescendos and effective diminuendos. The final two bars should set the seal on this exciting piece, a secure jump to the final chord making a stunning finale.

B:2 **Kabalevsky** Waltz (FL)

This beautiful but rather melancholy little waltz is one of the many gems in Kabalevsky's Op. 39. The RH's gently soaring phrases are delicately punctuated by the LH's light *sempre staccato* chords.

The RH phrases may be better understood and made secure if they are sung – with a breath at the end of each phrase. Shaping the phrases will naturally be achieved by following the written dynamics. The final diminuendo takes place over six bars and so it may be useful to mark in *mp* on the final beat of bar 26 before reaching *p* for the final two bars. Controlling this diminuendo and then the *rit.* from the upbeat to the final three bars will need practice, and at the end both wrists are gently lifted to produce a quiet staccato finish. The LH chords need to be practised separately at first, students listening to ensure that they play the chords lightly, evenly and clearly, accompanying rather than dominating the RH melody. In order that the higher RH notes do not lose their tone, fourth and fifth fingers need to be kept strong.

An appropriate balance of sound might be achieved by first singing the RH melody and then listening for it 'singing out' when the piece is played hands together. Watching a waltz on YouTube or TV dance programmes may help in realizing the dance's grace and elegance.

B:3 Vitalij Neugasimov Lazy Bear   FL

Born in 1978 in Vilnius, Lithuania, the composer Vitalij Neugasimov is well-known in that country as an organist, harpsichordist and teacher. His *Piano Sketches* books are proving very popular with students.

The LH fingers should be kept firm in order to project the melody over the RH chords. Here it helps to think of a lumbering bear and communicate all the articulation marks, especially the difference between accented notes and tenuto notes (meaning that notes are held for their full value). A quiz matching symbol to meaning to fill any gaps in knowledge can be followed by slow LH-only practice to embed the detail. In order that the RH quaver and staccato chords are crisp, they could first be practised on the piano lid. Keeping fingers closer to the keys will help passages marked *p*. Teacher and student might also play the piece as a duet, taking one hand each. Slow hands-together practice in short sections, counting in quavers, will help in delivering all the articulation. Isolated practice of bars 15–16 leading back to the beginning will enable a smooth da capo.

Discussing the 'lazy bear' and his activities is an initial step in conveying the character. The LH can really enjoy the piano's lower reaches as the RH chords punctuate the bear's ambling. The LH is not aimless, though, and good projection of the accents (at different dynamics) and the other articulation will help to highlight the bear's direction of movement.

B:4 Beethoven Nel cor più   FL

This is the Theme from Beethoven's Six Variations on 'Nel cor più non mi sento' – a duet from Paisiello's opera *L'amor contrastato* (1788). The RH's flowing $\frac{6}{8}$ melody is accompanied by broken chords in the LH.

There are many opportunities for RH/LH work and teacher-student duets in this lovely piece. Securing the LH can be enjoyably achieved by some solid practice in chords and possibly memorizing short sections before playing them with the RH, and then with both hands as written. Clapping the RH rhythms – again in short sections – will make playing them so much easier. A down-and-up wrist action will help to produce the two-note slurs. Balance of hands is important in what is essentially a song, and this can be illustrated in a game, by first playing the music with an overpowering LH. At this it will become very clear that a better way is needed, with a singing RH cantabile and a LH that is a discreet accompaniment.

'Nel cor più' is marked *dolce* throughout, even during the crescendos and the *f*, so encouraging students to listen to themselves and guard against harsh notes will help to maintain the song's delicate sound.

B:5 **Gurlitt** Night Journey (FL)

Cornelius Gurlitt was a nineteenth-century German composer who wrote many well-crafted and characterful piano pieces. 'Night Journey' is exciting and passionate with its strong bass melody and RH accompaniment of repeated chords. An imaginative and dramatic approach will bring it alive.

Bringing out and shaping the phrases of the LH is vital and may be accomplished by singing the phrases – breathing at the end of each one, playing with heavier fingers, transferring the weight from finger to finger to maintain the legato – and following the rises and falls as indicated by the hairpin dynamics. Focusing on keeping the fingers closer to the keys will help the RH to remain under the dynamic level of the LH.

The title 'Night Journey' conjures up several vivid scenarios: what sort of journey, where are they going, how are they travelling? These are all questions that will help to secure the dynamics and add to a descriptive performance. An andante tempo makes everything quite achievable at this grade, and a slowing down in the final bars will indicate the end of the journey. Schubert's song 'Erlkönig' has a similar sense of urgency and listening to it might help students grasp the dramatic mood that pervades this piece from beginning to end.

B:6 **Somervell** Plaintive Waltz (FL)

This delightful little D minor waltz by Arthur Somervell is from a collection entitled *Holiday Pictures*. Here it is tempting to think of a child rather regretfully finishing his or her holiday and heading back to school with a bit of a sigh.

The first section features a gently descending chromatic melody in the LH. Encouraging students to play this with heavier fingers should produce just the right sound. The second section, with two voices in the RH, includes several bars that are effectively in three parts. Students will need reminding to hold on the dotted minims and create the three-part harmonies (marking arrows on the score may help here). Securing the rather stretchy fingering of RH bars 14–16 might be achieved by first saying the fingering out loud; and here the forearm, hand and fingers need to be aligned in order to avoid undue emphasis on the thumb. The RH chords of the coda (bar 17–end) might appear less daunting once students are aware that an A sits at the top of each chord before a gentle descent in the last three bars. The *rit.* is helpful here too!

Talking about the meaning of 'plaintive' (slightly sad, melancholy, sorrowful, etc.) may contribute to establishing the mournful character of the waltz and help convey its gentle and subtle dynamics and changes of pace.

C:1 June Armstrong Dusty Blue

June Armstrong composes imaginative, original and pianistic music for developing pianists. 'Dusty Blue' comes from her *Paint Box* collection and will appeal to those who enjoy jazz-inspired music.

The piece presents no difficult rhythms for the RH, nor any awkward jumps, and only one hand moves position at any time. The LH moves through tonic-subdominant-tonic-dominant-subdominant-tonic positions in a typical 12-bar-blues bass line. This should be kept solid to create a 'heavy' blues sound (a bass guitar playing this LH line can be imagined) with a leisurely pulse. The RH quavers are to be 'swung' and the ornaments treated rather like guitar slides. A good legato touch should be employed for the melody, to contrast with the bass line, which needs to be detached but not staccato.

There are no dynamic markings given, so different dynamics may be explored to find out what works to create a really bluesy atmosphere (some further listening to typical blues music may help here). Making the final *molto rit.* really slow up at the end, and emphasizing those final two chords, will give a truly blues feel to the music.

C:2 B. Carleton Ja-Da

'Ja-Da' by Bob Carleton was composed in 1918 and quickly became a hit. It has flourished as a jazz standard, widely performed by many artists and bands, including Oscar Peterson, Frank Sinatra and The Pointer Sisters, and it also featured in a *Tom and Jerry* cartoon. This version, arranged by jazz pianist and composer Nikki Iles, is catchy and lively and will appeal to students who enjoy music with a jazzy flavour.

After two introductory bars, the music proper begins, following the lyrics of the original 'Ja-Da, Ja-Da, Ja-Da, Ja-Da, Jing, Jing, Jing' through bars 3–6. It may be helpful to sing the lyrics along with the melody to help with the syncopated rhythms. The melody lies comfortably under the hand and any leaps in the LH are preceded by rests which will give the player time to prepare for the next note.

The staccato chords are marked to be played 'cheekily', so the staccato should be bright and crisp. The melody has swung quavers, which gives the music a cheerful swagger. Details in the LH, such as in bars 6 and 21, can be highlighted to add interest and contrast. In addition to the articulation, the dynamics and harmonies really add to the character of this music so should be observed carefully, targeting clean execution of all the chords.

C:3 **Brian Chapple** Petite valse (Little Waltz) (FW)

Brian Chapple is an English composer whose attractive, accessible music is popular with early and intermediate piano students.

This 'little waltz' has an attractive legato melody with a chordal accompaniment, reminiscent of a waltz in a Tchaikovsky ballet. The melody lies comfortably under the fingers most of the time which will enable a smooth, sweet sound. The RH takes the melody first, the LH taking it over from bar 17. In each case, the melody needs to be clear, and the appropriate balance between the hands will be achieved by separate-hands practice. Marked Andante, the piece should feel leisurely but not dragging. Trying a 'plucked' staccato technique will help create a light touch and tone for the chords. Careful counting will ensure that the dotted rhythms (e.g. in bar 4) are played in time. The jumps between the chords, for example in bars 17–18 and 21–2, may present a challenge, so careful practice is needed to ensure accurate arrival on the higher chord.

Although there are only a handful of dynamic markings, there is scope in this music for some expressive shaping of the phrases. Students can be encouraged to think about the contour of each phrase and adjust the dynamics accordingly. A slowing down of the tempo from bar 29, together with the diminuendo, will bring this characterful piece to a gentle close.

C:4 **Gillock** A Memory of Paris (FW)

American composer William Gillock (1917–93) was affectionately called 'the Schubert of children's composers' as a tribute to his melodic skill. This evocative little waltz with a simple but elegant melody has a special warmth and stylishness, and will particularly appeal to students with sophisticated tastes.

The melody, shared between RH and LH, should feel smooth, supple and fluent: really secure fingering and a feeling of connection to the keys will achieve this. Your student should be sure to hold the dotted crotchets for their full value and to avoid shortening the notes marked with a pause (e.g. in bar 12). The staccato chords should be in time (this is a waltz, after all), light and delicate. The pedal in bars 15–16 and 31–4 adds warmth and resonance. In the closing bars, good coordination of the hands and security in the positioning of each duplet will allow the phrase to flow.

There is plenty of scope for expression here – imagine a carefree couple waltzing around a beautiful Parisian salon. The dynamics naturally follow the melodic rise and fall, while changes in tempo, which suggest rubato, further enhance the nostalgic atmosphere of this music: the piquant harmonies should be enjoyed, particularly the suspensions (e.g. in bar 8). The final bars suggest an improvised little coda, the music – and the memory – fading away to nothing.

C:5 **Saint-Saëns** Royal March of the Lion (FW)

The Carnival of the Animals, from which this piece is taken, is one of Saint-Saëns's most popular works, originally written as a bit of fun for the composer's friends. This grand march conjures up the size and stature of the lion, complete with menacing roars portrayed by chromatic scales (bars 9–10 and 13–14). Encourage students to listen to the orchestral original to hear how different instruments are used for dramatic effect.

As this is a march, a firm pulse is needed throughout the piece: it should feel imposing and majestic, particularly in the opening. Clear articulation, with good attention to details such as crisp staccato and accents, will enhance the character of the music. Pedalling right through bars 9–10 and 13–14 (the lion's roar) will create a dramatic, resonant tone. A clean, focused sound in the RH chords in bars 11 and 15 will suggest brass fanfares which contrast with the roars. At bar 17 the melody moves into a higher register with a softer dynamic; this is mirrored in the LH from bar 21, now marked *f* for dramatic effect.

Despite its apparently serious tone, there is definitely a 'tongue-in-cheek' mood to this piece. Students should be encouraged to explore ways of making the music sound both pompous and humorous, which will lead to a characterful and enjoyable performance.

C:6 **Pam Wedgwood** Lazy Days (FW)

The relaxed jazz-ballad style of this piece from popular composer and arranger Pam Wedgwood will appeal to students of all ages. The title and direction 'unhurried', together with the gentle syncopation in LH and RH in bars 1–8 (and later in bars 19–24) and jazz-infused harmonies, immediately suggest the lazy mood and tempo of this piece. The notes lie comfortably under the fingers and hand with no awkward jumps, and there is plenty of potential for expressive playing.

Careful counting will ensure that the syncopated notes fall in the right place, and a firm pulse with no hint of rushing will keep the third beat in time. Using good legato fingering – such as 5/2 and 4/1 – will help create a smooth transition between the RH chords in bars 1–7 and 19–24. At bar 11 the LH takes the melody; good balance between the hands, with light staccato RH chords, should be achieved by practising this section hands separately.

The aim is for a relaxed, easy-going atmosphere, enjoying the changing harmonies in the RH, both in the introductory bars and in the middle section's staccato chords. Students shouldn't hold back on expression: some variation in the dynamics in the opening section will create interest and colour, and allow the quavers in the penultimate bar to sound improvised.

GRADE 3

A:1 **Hook** Allegro

James Hook was a contemporary of Beethoven (they both died in the same year) but his music tends to be more 'early Classical' in style than that of Beethoven. It remains a popular choice for beginning and early intermediate pianists, and this light-hearted and rhythmic movement from one of his keyboard sonatinas is typical of his style. The middle section of the rounded binary form passes briefly through minor-key territory before building to a climax at bars 19-20, heralding the return of the opening material.

Precision and note accuracy will help achieve a sparkling performance of this piece, and a good fingering scheme in both hands will undoubtedly help with this. The LH accompaniment should be light but focused – imagining a bassoon playing this part will be helpful, aiming for a non-legato touch in the quavers. This will ensure that the leaps are managed comfortably, providing a good contrast to the semiquaver runs in the RH which should be even and rhythmic. Students should note the change into the treble clef for the LH in bars 9-12.

All dynamics and slurs are editorial suggestions only, so encourage your student to experiment with different articulation and dynamics, all with the aim of achieving a lively, characterful performance. As a general rule, the dynamics in repeated phrases (e.g. bars 5-8) can be altered for greater contrast. In the middle section, the ascending motion of the music suggests a crescendo before a dramatically contrasting *p* in bars 17-18.

A:2 **Seixas** Giga

The virtuoso organ and harpsichord player Carlos de Seixas was also the leading Portuguese composer of his time, and is known now mainly for his keyboard sonatas. His Giga (or Gigue) is typical of the genre – a fast, lively Baroque dance movement in compound time in two sections, with even quavers and a lilting character.

The RH carries the melody in this piece and the LH has a simple accompaniment, all of which lies comfortably under the hands. To retain the lively dance character, the aim should be for consistent fingering in the RH to achieve note accuracy and security. Imagining cellos or woodwind playing the LH with slight detachment between each chord or note will be useful here. This will also help with the octave leaps in bar 13 and bars 17-19. In bars 7-8 a sense of separate voices between the RH and LH quavers will add interest and contrast, while the notes in bar 11, which are shared between the hands, should feel like a single gesture with even quavers.

The mood of the piece changes several times throughout, which is reflected in the dynamics. These are editorial suggestions, as are the slurs, so students can be encouraged to experiment with different dynamics and articulation to create a performance that is stylistically authentic and characterful. A fractional delay before arriving at the *sf* RH notes in bars 9 and 20 will add extra emphasis.

A:3 M. Praetorius Bransle de la torche

Although primarily a composer of religious music, Michael Praetorius also wrote a set of dances called *Terpsichore*, from which this bransle, a dance popular in France in the Renaissance period, is taken. The word 'bransle' or 'branle' comes from the French verb *branler* meaning to shake or sway, and a bransle was danced by a chain of dancers, with linked arms or holding hands. The music is in the Dorian mode and displays harmonies (open 4ths and 5ths, for example) typical of early Renaissance music.

The piece is in binary form, with varied repeats. It starts out with a simple melody and a basic accompaniment, which switches between the hands from bar 9. The repeated staccato notes in the second half of each bar suggest the movement of the dancers' feet. From bar 17 the melody becomes more involved, with the introduction of quaver figures creating a greater sense of movement. The sustained lower notes in, for example, bars 1–6 form a simple melody which can be highlighted using a firm but not too emphatic touch.

A good underlying pulse is essential, while the melody should feel light and dance-like – really lifting the staccato notes out of the keyboard. From bar 17 the music starts to build towards the final climax, and arpeggiated chords from bar 25 create a real sense of grandeur. Even at *f*, the music should be kept light and dancing, with a final flourish in the last chord.

A:4 Dittersdorf English Dance in B flat

Dances were all the rage in the eighteenth century, and the 'English dance' was a popular form at this time, second only to the minuet. Less formal than the minuet, the English dance was normally in $\frac{2}{4}$ or $\frac{6}{8}$, and would have been danced in groups rather than couples. Austrian composer Carl Ditters von Dittersdorf (1739–99), one of the most prolific and versatile of Haydn's and Mozart's Viennese contemporaries, wrote a set of 20 English Dances for keyboard.

As it is a dance, a clear sense of pulse is needed throughout the piece, together with close attention to the articulation in order to create a lively character (the RH semiquavers in bar 7 should, by implication, be slurred in the same way as those in the penultimate bar). It is a good idea to imagine a bassoon playing the LH and aim for a clear focused sound. Allowing the quavers to be detached rather than staccato should also make the leaps and octaves easier to manage. The RH's 3rds in the middle section should not pose too many difficulties provided that a consistent fingering scheme is used.

 Although no tempo marking is given, a brisk rather than fast allegro would be appropriate for the character of the music, and a bright, confident tone with good attention to the dynamic contrasts (for example, bars 4–5 and 6–7) will really highlight the upbeat mood of this piece.

A:5 Haydn German Dance (FW)

Austrian composer Joseph Haydn was one of the most prolific and prominent composers of the Classical period. He wrote many symphonies, string quartets, choral works and piano sonatas, in addition to many shorter piano pieces which remain perennially popular, of which this German Dance is a good example. The German dance or ländler, a dance in three time, was the precursor to the waltz. It was a dance for pairs of dancers, and strongly featured hopping and stamping, and even some yodelling!

This jolly dance in G major is in straightforward ternary form, the return of the A section at bar 16 being a repeat of the opening section. With a marking of *Moderato ben ritmo*, the tempo should be not too fast but rhythmical with a clear three-in-a-bar pulse. Crisp staccato chords throughout in the LH lend a sprightly air to the piece and contrast with the long second phrase in the RH which should be smooth and shapely. The B section moves briefly into minor-key territory and presents a contrasting change in mood and dynamic. The return of the A section material should feel joyful and upright – remembering that this is music intended to be danced to.

Clearly defined articulation and a good sense of the change of key and mood in the B section will produce a performance that is characterful and true to the dance style.

A:6 Mozart Menuett in F (FW)

This sparkling little Menuett is dated 5 July 1762 and despite being composed when Mozart was still a young boy, the work offers sophisticated contrasting textures and rhythms in its use of triplets and semiquavers, and shows an awareness of writing for the harpsichord. Characteristically, a menuett has a moderate allegretto tempo and a cheerful feel with a clear sense of three beats in a bar.

The triplets should feel graceful and be given dynamic shaping as the music rises up the register. Keeping a clear sense of pulse throughout will ensure the switch to the semiquavers in bar 5 loses none of the underlying metre of the music. Here some rotary movement in the wrist and consistent fingering will give the semiquavers vitality and lightness and suggest harpsichord articulation and tone. Students might aim for LH quavers that are detached but not overly staccato – imagining, for each note, a cellist just touching the strings with the bow. Taking note of the change of dynamics is important, both here and at the return to *mf* in bar 9. The appoggiatura in bar 10 should be treated in exactly the same way as the final bar.

The brilliance of this piece comes from the different textures and changes in dynamics and articulation. Close attention to these details will result in an engaging and stylistically appropriate performance.

B:1 — **W. Carroll** Shadows

The exquisite children's pieces of Walter Carroll have proved popular choices for generations of developing players, and it is easy to understand why: Carroll had a remarkable talent for sketching appealing yet pedagogically useful music within modest frameworks. 'Shadows', an archetypical example, is a 30-bar impressionistic miniature that may introduce young players to pedalling for the first time.

Controlling the sustaining pedal is essential for success, and students should aim for quick reflexes when changing pedal at the beginning of the second beats in bars 1–3 and 9–12, but avoiding accentuations resulting from overly energetic footwork! Something to beware of is tension in the RH's thumb joints. Lifting these melody notes out of the keyboard while the pedal sustains the sonorities can be practised initially without the other RH notes (quavers); when the two elements are brought together, it will also help to work on the quaver line alone with no pedal but using a legato touch in which notes overlap for a little longer than their written notated values.

The tonal balance is important in every bar, and the beautiful expansiveness of this piece can be celebrated by allowing the pedal to create the impressionistic haze that is implied through the longer pedal markings from bar 13 onwards. Listening carefully to the chord formations at the end of each bar before continuing to play might prove a stimulating exercise, encouraging a greater awareness of tone quality and phrasing.

B:2 — **Gurlitt** Allegretto grazioso

Cornelius Gurlitt is mainly remembered as the composer of many short, attractive pieces, a number of which are regularly used as educational music. This charming waltz is especially beguiling, its melodic line and rhythmic accompaniment simple yet memorable.

The LH part offers an opportunity to develop finger-legato playing. By carefully holding down the first beat in the LH to the end of the second beat in each bar, it is possible to cultivate a 'finger-pedal' technique that affords a little more resonance than if the crotchets were realized exactly as written. In the RH in bars 17–22 the quavers may also be overlapped slightly in order to create more tonal warmth. In bars 21–2 silent practice on the surface of the keys may help in becoming familiar with the third finger's energetic activities. It is important to avoid mid-bar accents here.

The music will benefit from being felt as one-in-a-bar, and keeping the second and third beats light and accent-free will give a lilting feel. The move from p to $\textit{mf}$ in the central section can be celebrated – and a more strongly projected LH will provide textural contrast. The poetic, graceful atmosphere of the outer sections will be maintained by gently leaning on rather than overtly emphasizing each bar's first note. The hushed, gentle characterization has a vocal quality as well as a rhythmic basis so it may be helpful to sing the melodic line away from the piano in preparation for practising.

B:3 Reinecke Prelude

The prolific German composer Carl Reinecke had an innate understanding of the piano which is very evident in this charming Prelude. It is a study in arpeggiated figurations which is excellent for developing coordination and tonal balance.

The aim will be to keep the RH thumb relaxed and accent-free throughout. It plays on the second semiquaver of the first beat in virtually every bar and avoiding an accent here will require attention and careful listening. It may help to prepare each group of three RH notes in advance by placing the RH on the keyboard, then 'lifting' the fingers off the notes as they are played. In contrast, the LH needs more weight, relaxing the whole arm and allowing it to support the bass melody line as it unfolds. Pedalling lightly in between each of the beats in the LH would work well.

The music's character is certainly not agitated, and time to breathe should be taken every four bars so that the music maintains a sense of grandeur. The LH's nobility is best served by using a rich tonal range. This might mean experimenting with a stronger dynamic level than is indicated on the score. In contrast the RH needs a much quieter approach. Listening for and deciding on tonal balance between the hands will help in building the character of the piece.

B:4 L. Cohen Hallelujah

Leonard Cohen's universally loved song seems destined for even more widespread popularity in this attractive arrangement by Carolyn Miller. The words given beneath the melody line – apart from encouraging singing at the piano

– may also help to build harmonic awareness: in bars 14–16 the lyrics describe the actual chord sequence of those bars.

Crossing the second finger over the thumb in the LH arpeggio patterns commonly causes anxiety and physical stiffness. Working at each LH bar independently can therefore encourage more confidence and lead to greater facility, especially if each bar is seen at first as an independent 'exercise'. Practising quietly with many repetitions with eyes closed could prove to be very helpful. This piece also offers a wonderful opportunity to develop confidence with pedalling. Again, this can be developed by working initially with the LH alone. Not every note need be bathed in sonority (with pedal employed from the first to last notes of every bar); if the pedal is depressed at the beginning of each bar it can be released for the bar's last two notes. This approach works for each bar in the piece, enabling a sense of calm continuity and ease to be built up.

The words can help shape the performance throughout, and it may be helpful to sing the melodic line internally while playing. Within the given dynamic markings it is possible to add further shading. The 'growing intensity' stipulated at the beginning can be seen as a gradual build-up to the *mf* section in bars 21–8.

B:5 **Martha Mier** Thistles in the Wind

Martha Mier's popularity with younger pianists is understandable. She has a talent for memorable, evocative characterization and mood painting within a popular twentieth-century style that often encompasses the jazz music of her native America.

Control and confidence in the LH (bars 1–12) can be built up if it is practised on its own at a *f*, even a *ff*, dynamic level – provided that the melodic shape is always considered. Students can try singing the melody out loud while playing the LH, then adding the RH at as quiet a level as possible. Gradually students can balance their hands with more subtlety, but there should always be a sense that the LH is more sonorous than the RH. Bars 13–22 work in reverse to the opening half of the piece! Here an overlapping finger-legato technique will enhance the RH touch and, again, the tonal balance between the hands requires skilful coordination, but can be refined through practising the RH at a much louder level than the LH.

Tonal beauty, lilting rhythms and a sense of serenity are all to be cultivated and strived for in this charmingly wistful miniature, which is made even more bewitching in the final line through a wash of sustaining pedal and a bell-like final top F. This last note should be celebrated and cherished – a proverbial cherry on the cake which adds a final soupçon of magic!

B:6 · Tchaikovsky · Old French Song

This well-loved piece has memorable melodic content, gentle characterization, and delicate, idiomatic textures in the accompaniment. As with so many of Tchaikovsky's easier piano pieces there is a tremendous range of colour to explore – and from the beginning the piano is turned into a virtual orchestra.

Care should be taken not to begin too quietly. The RH, even at *p*, has a strong melodic content and needs to project with conviction over the LH. Practising at *mf* with relaxed arm movements and wrists, ensuring that each note overlaps with the next, will be helpful. The *pp* from the upbeat to bar 9 should feel tension-free. Using arm weight to control the softer dynamic should also prove useful. Though the pedal is not necessary, its subtle deployment after each dotted crotchet (bars 2, 4, 8, etc.) may help to unify the phrasing. If pedal is used here, less of it rather than more is preferable: depressing it immediately after the dotted crotchet in, for example, bar 2 then releasing it just after playing the bar's final quaver will be both discreet and effective.

This piece is typical of much Russian music in that it essentially flows in one continuous musical unit. Thinking of the RH as a single long phrase, giving a bird's-eye view of the complete melodic shape, will minimize the risk of over-accentuation in the melody, and of over-emphasizing the breaks between phrases, which might easily become disconnected. Phrase beginnings and endings can be projected with subtle inflections and seen less as breaks in the melody than as colouristic opportunities to enjoy.

C:1 · Bartók · Dance

Bartók's *For Children* ranks alongside Schumann's *Album for the Young* and Bach's *Little Preludes* as some of the most effective piano music for developing pianists. This Dance has the repetitious nature and narrow melodic range that is typical of Slovakian folk tunes. There are fewer notes to learn than might at first appear – with the RH question-and-answer phrases being repeated three times!

The LH rhythm might be introduced as a percussion or clapping accompaniment as the teacher plays the RH melody. This could then progress to playing short sections of the chords as the teacher again plays the melody before the student brings both hands together and increases the speed. The RH melody is given interest by the variety of articulation marks, which should be conveyed precisely as on the score. The RH fingering enables fluent playing but is occasionally unexpected, and circling these fingerings may provide a helpful reminder. Playing slowly and counting four quavers in the early stages should help to secure the independence of hands needed and build confidence.

The piece can look a little daunting on the page, but understanding where the RH melody repeats, and what kind of changes there are on each repetition, might help to combat this. In addition, watching a performance of a Slovakian czardas online, or listening to a recording of one, should contribute towards an understanding of this quiet but beautiful dance.

C:2 **R. R. Bennett** Diversion (FL)

This playful and humorous Diversion is one of a suite of seven short characterful pieces. Its cheeky character is expressed through swift changes of articulation and dynamics ranging from *pp* to *f*. The $\frac{3}{8}$ time signature and constant quavers keep it moving ever onwards and dancing down the next musical path or diversion.

A good first step will be to identify the main theme in bar 1 and subsequent reappearances. Slow separate-hands practice in short phrases (e.g. bars 1–3, and 3–7) will bring familiarity with the articulation and dynamics, with special attention being paid to the LH 3rds. Observing the recommended fingering is necessary for effective staccato and legato 3rds. While it might be tempting to play the RH more than the LH, practising passages with the LH then the RH and then the LH again should redress the balance and result in a confident sound as the LH alternately accompanies or cheekily replies to the RH.

Realizing the full range of dynamics and different articulation required and remembering that Giocoso means 'playful' or 'humorous' will help to give this piece its quirky style. Moving the LH in the penultimate bar, ensuring that fingers are in position just above the notes and firm as the wrist gently presses down, will help convey the atmospheric ending of the final low *pp* chord.

C:3 **Nikki Iles** Blues in the Attic (FL)

This specially commissioned soulful blues solo from Nikki Iles suggests that the attic might be the place to go to reflect and try out new musical ideas. The piano becomes drum, bass and possibly saxophone soloist as it revels in luscious dissonances and funky rhythms. Those players with a feel for the blues and a strong sense of rhythm may especially enjoy learning and performing this delicious piece.

Seeing the music as a jazz trio could be the key to interpretation – beginning with the LH as the rock-solid drum and bass then placing the RH saxophone soloist on top to play and explore the chromatic blues melodies. The three main sections and coda might also be tried as a teacher-student duet, thereby securing one hand but hearing the other at the same time. It might also be useful to clap, play and possibly memorize the LH middle section with its satisfying pattern of 5ths. The often syncopated rhythms of the RH and the LH are best worked on by first clapping and counting and then playing and counting short phrases.

The middle section, marked More relaxed, presents the opportunity to relax the speed a little before, after a little break in the sound, returning at bar 17 to the ideas and tempo of the opening section. Students often imagine that they are achieving a crescendo when it is not in fact heard, so asking a friend or family member to listen and try to identify crescendos will be a useful exercise.

C:4 June Armstrong Unicorn (Monocerus) FL

June Armstrong, who lives in Northern Ireland, composes piano music that specifically focuses on atmospheric playing, and the development of a tonal palette and a sensitive pedalling technique. Her motto is 'Music of the Imagination'. Armstrong describes this as a magical piece about a magical creature. It has a Debussyesque character and learning it will reward students who take an imaginative approach.

The notes of the piece range over what could be a daunting four octaves; however, most of the LH has a relatively narrow span and is easier to read, making it a good starting point. Explaining the meaning of 8va and 15ma and working out where these RH notes are on the keyboard is a logical next step, leaving the last two bars where the hands climb higher as the final activity in the note-learning process. Adding the *tre corde* pedal adds depth and colour to the whole piece, producing a magical ethereal effect; an atmospheric performance will benefit from observing the pedal signs and also from very careful listening.

Armstrong suggests that we try to imagine the grace and aloofness of the unicorn. The unicorn is also a constellation (*monocerus* is Greek for unicorn), so imagining a dark night sky with twinkling pinpoint stars in the shape of a unicorn will help students to create the delicate touch and sensitive balance needed to bring this particular unicorn to life.

C:5 Lerner and Loewe Wouldn't it be Loverly? FL

This song was written for the 1956 Broadway play *My Fair Lady*, subsequently made into a film in 1964 starring Audrey Hepburn as a cockney flower girl. It looks quite long but students will be delighted to find that the opening is repeated!

Articulation is clearly marked with slurs, staccato notes, and so on, but where no slurs are marked a stylish effect may be achieved by gently detaching notes. Saying aloud 'down-up' as hands do exactly that in bars 5–6 and 23–4 will help to embed the gesture needed to produce two-note slurs. Although it might be tempting to release the LH fifth-finger semibreves in the coda, thinking of a weight in the fifth finger should discourage this, as well as drawing a line to the end of the bar. If the optional small-note triplet in bars 12 and 18 is included, care must be taken not to slacken the pace of the melody. In the final four bars there is a rare appearance of the *una corda* pedal, which will produce an automatic echo.

Singing along to this popular song on YouTube or other recordings will greatly help familiarity. The arranger, Alan Bullard, suggests that it is performed while thinking of 'an excited, perky ... slightly apprehensive young lady dreaming of what the future might hold', and that the final 'loverly' is conveyed 'with a sense of mystery and quiet hope'.

C:6 **Christopher Norton** Face in the Crowd (FL)

This is a slightly sad little waltz, with a jazz feel. It seems to describe someone glimpsing a friend's face in the crowd but the friend frustratingly slips away before there's the chance to say hello. The pace is one-in-a-bar and within that there are opportunities for expressive touches of rubato.

Counting quavers in the early stages of learning may help the overall pulse not to falter in those bars where LH quavers are grouped in duple time (bars 8 and 24). It will also be important to achieve a warm RH cantabile, and this can be accomplished by always keeping fingers in contact with the keys, listening carefully to judge the resulting sound. Pedalling depends on the individual player. If pedal is wished throughout, this might be once a bar, except for where marked in bar 8 (and bar 24), and in bars 11 and 12 where the pedal should be changed on each chord. However, it is also possible to use it just in bars 8 and 24. Practising the LH and its pedalling first before adding the RH may help.

The waltz overall is rather mellow, and that feeling will be created and maintained by starting p with gentle rise and fall in the LH, and using a warm rather than a harsh f at bar 13. Students can enjoy relaxing the tempo where marked, and allow the ending to settle gently by observing the *poco rit.* and the pause.

GRADE 4

A:1 **Beethoven** Bagatelle in C

Though Beethoven is most famous for his large-scale works, his bagatelles for piano show him to be a master of the miniature too. They are often charming, characterful and very concentrated, saying a tremendous amount within the shortest of time spans. This Bagatelle is a highly contrasted miniature with a central section that contains typically Beethovenian sforzandos in the RH.

The opening needs projection of the RH's top line. Practising the lower part staccato while keeping the upper part legato may help. When playing this section it is important to keep the wrist loose as stiffness inhibits fluency and may negatively affect tone quality. Stiffness in the wrists also must be avoided from bar 9. The C minor central section containing RH position changes requires fluidity, with no unwanted accentuation on the thumbs when changing position – eyes-closed practice could prove useful here.

It may be inspiring to imagine the opening bars realized by a sonorous string quartet. Pedalling in between each quaver beat may help maintain richness of tone and legato. The whole bagatelle can be given a sense of forward motion, with phrasing that encourages a feeling of graceful movement. In the Traurig section the fifth-finger notes might be held for longer than written in order to create a little more resonance; there is no need for pedal. Provided that a sense of cantabile is always present in the RH, the semiquavers may be either legato or *leggiero*. Throughout, care should be taken to keep the LH much quieter than the RH.

A:2 **Benda** Sonatina in A minor

The keyboard output from the Bohemian-born Georg Benda was enormous. His style shows the influence of his close friend C. P. E. Bach as well as dance elements that have clear roots in the Baroque suite. At the same time there are tantalizing glimpses of the Viennese Classics to come. While some bars of this sonatina movement show Baroque influences in terms of texture, it begins with an arpeggiated figure that immediately evokes the spirit of the Classical style.

Feeling comfortable with the numerous leaps between registers is important, so it will prove useful to practise the specific jumps in isolation. For the RH 6ths and 3rds in, for example, bars 2 and 4 the wrists should be kept loose, but students should aim for an economical technique with fingers close to the keys.

It may be helpful to use two-note slur groupings mixed with staccato for the semiquaver arpeggios and flourishes that permeate the piece. These might be conceived of as bow markings (staccatos equating to up-bows, slurs to down-bows). In these figurations the use of the sustaining pedal is best avoided. A *leggiero*, accent-free touch could make the semiquavers from bars 17 and 33 really sparkle. Keeping an energized, consistent pulse is important for structural cohesion, and players should be especially diligent over rhythmic discipline when the semiquavers abruptly stop in bar 40. Double dotting in the manner of a French Baroque overture may be a nice stylistic touch in bar 44.

A:3 Telemann Petit jeu (Little Game)

Georg Philipp Telemann was a celebrity composer of the Baroque era, but sadly his prolific output, including substantial works for keyboard, remains largely neglected today. This charmingly characterful piece, part of a larger keyboard collection in which fugues are contrasted with shorter homophonic pieces, shows characteristics of the polonaise in its ceremonial, processional character, in triple metre.

Cultivating a neat, crisp staccato and *leggiero* technique is important for both the tonal range and control in this piece. Students should strive to create compact, concentrated finger movements. It might be helpful to keep non-playing fingers relaxed but as still as possible. Facility in the semiquaver passages can be built up by practising in small units, keeping the focus on a finger's individual movement. Excellent clarity will be achieved if each finger moves quickly and remains as close to the keys as possible. The trills in bars 7 and 21 may be worked at in triplets, stopping on each quaver at first.

Tempo can be gauged from bars 7 and 21 where it is important to feel in control of the triplets. At the opening of the piece (and at the beginning of each section) the upbeat bar, with its three LH quavers, should not be given undue accentuation. LH articulation can be exclusively detached though it is also possible to experiment by adding slurs. In terms of dynamics there are so many possibilities that could work, as long as all is within the context of a light-hearted, non-legato aesthetic.

A:4 J. S. Bach Minuet

This Minuet is one of the most famous movements from J. S. Bach's Suites. It has an immediacy and dancing characterization, including figurations that seem idiomatic also on non-keyboard instruments, suiting a flautist's articulation or even a violinist's bowing.

Slow, methodical practice with consistent fingering will gradually build confidence and control. It may help to practise the (editorial) two-note slurred patterns in isolation, ensuring that there is economy of movement allied to coordination. This means ease in 'sitting' on the first note of each slur, followed by release at a quieter dynamic level on the second note. Different two-note fingerings for the slur patterns should be tried in order to see which works best. (In bars 2 and 4, try using the same two fingers for each pair of quavers in the RH. It is possible to finger each pair with 1-3, 2-4, or even 2-5 throughout.) Practising the whole piece staccato may also bring rewards. This could work effectively if too much arm weight is avoided. An appropriate touch may be adopted by keeping finger movements as small as possible with the hands close to the keyboard. 'Drawing' fingers towards the body should provide a convincing *leggiero* touch that avoids heaviness in the texture.

As in all Bach and other Baroque music, approaches to interpretation vary. There are no rules here, and recordings of this Minuet show a diverse range of tempos and choices of articulation. It is however necessary, of course, that there is a consistent pulse and that good overall control is maintained.

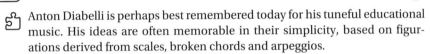

A:5 | Diabelli Scherzo: Allegro

Anton Diabelli is perhaps best remembered today for his tuneful educational music. His ideas are often memorable in their simplicity, based on figurations derived from scales, broken chords and arpeggios.

A good first step is to get to know the LH quaver figuration by playing the quavers in block triads. After that, slow and relaxed practice of the quavers will allow an even tone and consistency of articulation to develop. More colour and security will be possible in the RH if its *sf* notes in the bass clef are taken in the pedal (very quick up-down footwork on each bass-clef crotchet could be effective). It is an idea to practise all the RH crossing-hand leaps in any one session, working at each leap quietly and slowly, becoming aware of the physical movement required. Once this is more familiar, students can begin to play without looking at the keyboard. Crisp, coordinated articulation in the LH staccato triads from bar 17 will be achieved by a loose wrist; fingers should be kept close to the keyboard in this section, which can be built up gradually by working in small units.

This Scherzo is typical of Diabelli in that it demands energy, sparkle and clarity. It is a piece of contrasts: tonal contrasts between each hand (LH quavers to be kept in the background so that the charmingly energized RH takes centre stage); contrasts in articulation, such as between staccato, *sf* and legato; and striking dynamic contrasts, which are important to the overall characterization.

A:6 **Haydn** Finale: Presto

Haydn's extraordinary legacy is especially rich for pianists, and his keyboard sonatas encompass an enormous range and diversity of mood. Perhaps because there are so many in total (over 50, though opinions vary as to the exact number), several of Haydn's sonatas remain under-performed. The neglected A major Sonata, from which this movement comes, is typical of the composer at his most high-spirited and positive.

Once fingering is established, economy of finger movement can be empha-sized in separate-hands work that can be built up gradually in the first few weeks of preparation. Rotary movement in the RH in bars 11–12 could be helpful. Here, and throughout the passagework, there is a danger that thumb notes might be overly accented. 'Finger independence' unquestionably makes it easier to avoid unwanted accents, awkward shifts of position, and notes that fail to speak. Synchronizing scale passages between the hands at bars 6–7 and 22–3 may be easier if students avoid unnecessary movements from fingers that are not playing.

The Presto marking should not invoke panic, and the key is to find an ener-gized character without choosing an uncomfortable tempo! Dynamics can be creatively explored. Phrasing, too, is very much open to the individual: semiquavers might be divided into groups of four, with two notes slurred and two staccato, or three slurred with the fourth staccato. Either way, the lack of articulation on the score can be taken as an opportunity for experimentation.

B:1 **W. Carroll** The Reef

2019 marks the 150th anniversary of the birth of pioneering educational com-poser Walter Carroll, and it is a testament to his fertile musical imagination that his pieces continue to inspire and spark the enthusiasm of today's learners. 'The Reef' is a wonderful example of his picturesque and evocative writing. His vivid depiction of 'the great rock' in the ocean, with waves play-ing at its feet, is sure to prove a favourite and should elicit renewed interest in the collection from which it comes, *In Southern Seas*.

This piece could be used as an effective study in arm weight and flexibility. The opening *ff* chords, with accented staccato touch fully sustained by the damper pedal, can resound as magnificently as the instrument allows, but are contrasted by the subtler *p* fingerwork in bars 5–10 and again in bars 15–22, where pedalling can be applied with less depth, and used more to add warmth and tonal colour. It may prove instructive to use a metro-nome to check that the tempo in these softer bars is consistent with the opening chords.

The performance marking 'Massive' is a quirky indication of the monumental effect this piece should convey. There is plenty of musical detail to notice throughout, though, and effective contrasts will add to the dramatic imagery of the piece. Players should be sure to enjoy the suspense of bars 21–2 before launching into the grandiose ending!

B:2 **Grieg** Arietta (AE)

'Arietta' is the opening piece from Grieg's first collection of *Lyric Pieces* (published in 1867 as his Op. 12), and it is surely one of his most gorgeous piano miniatures – indeed one of the most beautiful pieces in the whole repertoire. It might be compared with his final *Lyric Piece*, entitled 'Remembrances' and written more than three decades later, which recalls the melody of the 'Arietta', transforming it into a nostalgic slow waltz – a touching reflection on this piece's immense and enduring popularity.

Players at Grade 4 level might not have previously encountered the three-part texture that dominates this piece but, once understood, the patterns fit nicely under the hand. Students should try isolating just the middle-line semiquavers, playing them *pp*. The LH in bar 6 includes a tricky stretch. Some may prefer to use finger 2 on the first G in the bar, keeping the thumb for middle C. Another option is to play the middle C with the RH. Whichever solution works best here, good control of legato pedalling will be needed, and this applies throughout.

'Arietta' can be performed effectively at quite a range of different tempos, and it is interesting to experiment with the limits of that range, aiming for delicacy of touch regardless of speed. Most importantly, the top line must remain cantabile, evoking the 'little song' of the piece's title, and absorbing the listener's full attention. This will require effective voicing of the inner parts.

B:3 **Elgar** Chanson de matin (Morning Song) (AE)

Elgar's evergreen *Chanson de matin* was composed for violin and piano, and has subsequently appeared in many arrangements, establishing itself as one of his most popular melodies. This solo piano arrangement stays remarkably true to Elgar's original, while also providing an accessible version for the intermediate pianist.

Separate RH practice will help develop attention to well-shaped phrasing. Producing a cantabile line is a priority, calling for effective legato fingering and applied arm weight. The passage from bar 31 onwards may require particular care; where there are two- or three-note chords, aim to keep the top melody dominant, using additional weight. The LH accompaniment needs to hold its minim bass notes, allowing the offbeat chords to gently murmur and lead the tempo forwards. In both hands, staccato notes should be played lightly, without accentuation or bounce.

 This is a piece of two halves – the first presenting the well-loved main tune, the second perhaps less familiar. Bar 23 is the key moment where this new section begins, with the melodic interest briefly in the LH. Making this moment special will ensure that the overall shape and structure is communicated. The allargando climax that follows in bars 31–2 can be much slower. When following the opening instruction of *con Ped.*, 'half pedalling' can be preferable in the first half of the piece, changing once per bar, but with generally less pedalling in the second half.

B:4 | Grechaninov In the Fields (AE)

This quirky delight comes from a collection of pieces entitled *Glass Beads*, written by the Russian piano teacher and composer Alexander Grechaninov and published in 1929. The 12 pieces in the set evoke the simple joys of childhood. 'In the Fields' has two contrasting musical ideas – one based on patterns and motion, the other more lyrical – and each is taken at a different tempo. Players might enjoy creating their own narrative for the piece: what is the story here? The gentle shifts from major to minor can feed the imagination!

The biggest challenge in this piece, with its frequent time signature and tempo changes, pauses, and LH rests on the first beat, is to maintain and communicate a clear sense of pulse. In the early stages of learning, counting out loud may help. Students should notice, too, that the marked phrases often go across the bar-line, and ideally these will have clarity in the performance.

Making the most of every expressive detail and contrast will enhance the 'story' that is told. Features to observe include the unexpected offbeat accents (e.g. bars 10 and 22), the dramatic use of pause bars, and occasional staccato for contrast. Rests given their full length will add clarity to the structure and the textural changes. The surprise appearance of the slower, lyrical folk-like melody from bars 24 and 44 will delight the listener, especially if played with an expressive cantabile. Effective dynamic contrasts in the final section will provide a magical ending.

B:5 | Kullak Grandmama Tells a Ghost Story (AE)

This grandmama is a brilliant storyteller, judging from this enjoyable miniature by the nineteenth-century German composer Theodore Kullak. A student of Czerny, Kullak followed his teacher's example, devoting much of his energy to teaching and writing educational music. 'Grandmama Tells a Ghost Story' comes from his second collection of 12 *Scenes from Childhood*, Op. 81, and remains one of his most popular compositions. Kullak's witty characterization and attention to detail help make the piece inspiring for students and a delight to teach.

🖐 This piece includes a few tricky moments that benefit from isolated work. The double 3rds (bar 4) are one such case, as are the RH chord passages in bars 7–8, for example, and 45–7. Balance can be a problem when the melody moves to the LH in bar 39 and needs to be projected clearly. The demisemi-quavers in the opening motif are highly effective if delivered exactly in the notated rhythm, rather than played more loosely.

🎨 The instruction *parlando* can be translated as 'like speech' or 'eloquent', and here suggests that a strong emphasis should be placed on the declamatory melody line, with due consideration given to the details of rhythm, articulation and expression. Pedal may be entirely avoided, other than where marked (bars 36–7 and 44–5). Suspense can be created by giving weight to the fermatas in bars 16 and 23, while great fun can be had with the dynamics in bars 16–19 and the accents throughout.

B:6 | **Tchaikovsky** Morning Prayer (AE)

📑 'Morning Prayer' is the beautiful opening piece from Tchaikovsky's popular *Album for the Young*, Op. 39, published in 1878 with the subtitle '24 Easy Pieces (à la Schumann)'. It evokes the sound of a choir at morning church, and until bar 16 the four-part texture falls under a typical SATB range. Students singing the parts will be alerted to the inner lines, which will inform good voicing of the chords at the piano.

🖐 Playing the chords smoothly and with a sense of legato inner voicing is a particular challenge of this piece. Success requires careful attention to fingering; suggestions given are editorial only, so alternatives can be considered. As always it is beneficial to practise without any pedal, listening to each of the four parts in turn. It may also help to play very slowly, pausing to learn the feel of unusual fingering patterns and stretches. LH practice from bar 16 may be necessary to tame a wayward little finger and develop rhythmic security in the bass line.

🎨 'Morning Prayer' has a simple arch shape, steadily building from a soft beginning to a climax at bar 12 before diminishing to the end. The mood can stay fairly calm throughout, but the best effect will be achieved if the dynamic shape is communicated with musical conviction. Pedalling is optional, but if it is used sparingly – and with care not to blur the many chromatic notes – it can add the warm glow that will truly lift a performance of this piece.

C:1   **Gillock**   Holiday in Paris

The twirling quavers with their waltz-inspired accompaniment lend a care-free air to this charming miniature. The piece is in ABA form with a contrasting middle section (from bar 16) and a long coda.

The RH quavers lie comfortably under the hand, mostly in a five-finger position which will assist in accuracy and effective legato playing. The lower note in the LH is sustained for two beats to create some interesting harmonies, and although the direction is to pedal through the entire bar, the LH notes need to be released on time. Experimenting with half-pedal, or even one-third, might be useful to avoid obscuring the quavers. At bar 16 the LH takes over the quavers and the texture changes, with no pedal and staccato chords in the RH; here a 'plucked' touch will create a bright, crisp sound. While it is not necessary to share the quavers between the hands, as marked, in bars 45–8, from bar 49 to bar 52 the sharing of the groupings between hands will be vital in order to create a rather attractive virtuosic flourish.

Good attention to the dynamic markings, changes in tempo, use of rubato and delicacy of touch, particularly in the quavers, will enhance the expressive qualities and quirky nature of this music. The changes in mood are generally led by the changing LH harmonies, so the player needs to be alert to differing musical colours and dynamics to suggest these subtle shifts.

C:2   **Richard Michael**   A Kwela for Caitlin

Kwela is a style of popular African music which has jazzy rhythms and a distinctive beat. This lively kwela by Scottish jazz musician and teacher Richard Michael has a melody of swung, offbeat quavers, often cut short by rests, varied repeats and clear articulation (accents and staccato) to create energy and drama. This piece will suit a student with a taste for jazz-inspired music and a good sense of rhythm.

A clear pulse will give the music a sense of forward propulsion. Except where specifically indicated, the notes should be played non-legato so that the slurred notes, when they occur, provide contrast and interest. Further contrast and vitality is created by the shifts between f and p: these changes need to be precise to maintain the drama of the music. There are many unison passages and these should be played with absolute clarity and precision. The rests need to be given their full value, particularly in places such as bars 10 and 12.

The music shifts from cheerful D major to B minor at bar 17, signalling a change of mood and musical colour. From bar 35 the rhythmic momentum and dynamic vitality need to be kept going: crisply articulated staccato chords contrast with smooth crotchets in the LH, with the final two bars creating a lively $f\!f$ climax, with accented RH chords and a rising quaver figure in the

LH. Observe all the articulation and be sure to give the crotchet rests in bars 40 and 41 their full value, to create additional drama.

C:3 **Luboš Sluka** Rytmická (Rhythmical)

This vibrant piece by Czech composer Luboš Sluka is a study in rhythm and a great test of independence of the hands.

The entire piece is underpinned by regular quaver chords, mostly in the LH, though the RH takes these over from bar 30. Marked staccato, they should be light and not too 'chugging': a 'plucked' staccato technique with the hands kept close to the keys will help create the right touch and sound, and will enable easy movement between the changing chords. Students should watch for the chord changes as these sometimes occur mid-bar (e.g. in bar 3). Meanwhile, the RH springs about the keyboard over this accompaniment, articulated with crisp staccato. Where the RH crosses over the LH, it will be useful to practise moving very quickly from one position to another, while keeping the tempo of the music slow. The rests should also be seen as opportunities to move into position ahead of striking the note. This will train quick reflexes and ensure notational accuracy when the music is played at full tempo. The rests in the final bars should be given their full value.

Aside from the strict sense of pulse, much of the character of this piece comes from the articulation. Dynamic markings are suggestions only, and the changes in harmony in the chords may inspire further dynamic colouring.

C:4 **Ben Crosland** Sleepytown Blues

Ben Crosland is a British musician, teacher and composer who writes mainly educational music in jazz and pop styles which is both inspiring and achievable. This accessible piece is a great example of why Crosland's music is so popular with children and adults alike.

The title and the direction 'Lazily' suggest the tempo, a leisurely four-in-a-bar. There is also a practical reason for this speed: there is some jumping around in the RH, and a good awareness of keyboard geography will help students manage these leaps (e.g. in bar 13). Practice strategies might include springing off the high note and travelling to low notes as quickly as possible to train reflexes. The opening has the flavour of an introduction, the RH triplets imitating a guitar 'bend', and they should feel relaxed and 'cool'. The accidentals, which fall comfortably under the fingers, should not present any problems. In bars 9–14 the LH adopts a typical blues-style bass riff, alternating between tonic (G) and subdominant (C) chords. The composer creates the sense of a swing rhythm in bars 9–14 through the LH crotchet/quaver groupings which match the RH triplets (explaining how they fit together will make the triplet groupings less daunting!). In these bars the high and low RH triplets can be treated as separate voices or instruments – perhaps a harmonica and blues guitar.

A relaxed, bluesy atmosphere with plenty of expression and rubato will result in an authentic and enjoyable performance.

C:5 Bernard Désormières Anatolian 08

Contemporary French composer and pianist Bernard Désormières is known for his brilliant jazz improvisations as well as fine performances of classical repertoire. Stylistically, this piece owes much to the swing genre of jazz, popularized by musicians such as Oscar Peterson, Nat King Cole and Ella Fitzgerald.

The direction above the metronome mark indicates that the RH quavers should be swung to create a lilting rhythm (*croches 'ternaires'* in bar 24 means the same thing). The RH melody has an improvisatory feel, with tied notes to create syncopation. The music's rhythmic beat is set by the LH and students should aim to maintain a clear pulse throughout. The lower note of the octaves may be omitted if the stretch proves too big, and students might give a weighty yet accurate attack in the LH, to give the chords a fuller texture. When combined with the pedal this suggests a big-band sound. Bearing in mind that this is jazz, the ornaments should have an improvisatory character and not feel too metronomic. The tremolo in the final chord can be created by alternating between the hands as quickly as possible.

The piece is in ternary form with clear delineation between the sections. In a convincing performance, the melody will have an extemporized feel (though within a steady pulse), and, because of the music's repetitive nature, it needs changes in colour and dynamics. Rests (e.g. in bar 32) should be given their full value to create added drama.

C:6 Prokofiev Peter's Theme

Peter and the Wolf, Prokofiev's 'fairy tale for children', is one of the best-loved and most frequently performed works in the entire classical repertoire. Each character of the tale is represented by a corresponding instrument in the orchestra. Peter's Theme, which beautifully evokes a confident, happy-go-lucky boy, is usually played by orchestral strings, and this arrangement retains key elements of the original – an attractive melody set over a moving bass line.

The primary technical challenges lie in successfully coordinating the RH melody with the legato LH accompaniment. Good fingering and wrist flexibility will help here: students can be encouraged to use lateral arm movement and allow the second or third finger of each quaver group to act as a pivot around which the rest of the hand moves. This will also help those with smaller hands manage the LH part. The melody needs clear articulation and a good sense of the dotted rhythms when they appear. Plenty of separate-hands practice will ensure that both parts are well learnt. The final bars are unison scales and should be firm and precise with good attention to dynamics.

By listening to the original of this charming piece students will gain further insights into its character and mood. It is also worth noting how the instrumentation is organized to offer ideas about voicing and articulating the phrases. The melody should be playfully boyish and confident, with a clear sense of four-in-a-bar throughout.

GRADE 5

A:1   J. S. Bach   Aria

J. S. Bach's Six Partitas (published as *Clavierübung*, Part 1 in 1731) are a milestone in the keyboard repertoire, each comprising a series of movements in a range of Baroque dance genres. This Aria comes from the fourth partita in the set, and although the title might suggest it to be a slow piece (as is the famous Aria from the *Goldberg Variations*), it is in fact a sprightly and characterful dance, with perky syncopations and bravura runs in both hands.

The texture comprises two-part counterpoint, preparation for which might include exploring Bach's easier Two-Part Inventions. These mostly have simpler implied harmony, which will stimulate aural development. In this particular aria it will help to analyze the harmonic progressions and modulations, taking particular care in the passage from bar 25 to bar 32, where there are some unexpected twists! The LH jumps beginning in bar 41 will benefit from careful practice separately, and even with eyes shut, to develop consistent accuracy. Although pedalling is generally unnecessary, it may help to use a brief touch on the recurring low As in bars 41–4, mimicking the resonance of the low harpsichord strings, releasing on the second quaver each time.

While this piece must not drag, setting too quick a tempo at the start may prove difficult to maintain. Energy can be added by using crisp articulation, but making sure to include differences of touch. Dynamics are left to the performer – some variety here will contribute positively to the overall shape of the piece. Emphasizing the syncopated offbeat movement of the opening theme can also add *brio* to the movement.

A:2   Haydn   Andante in A

This charming Classical Andante by Haydn is in fact an abridged transcription of the second movement from his popular Symphony No. 53, 'L'impériale'. Listening to a recording of the original orchestral version will help to establish a sense of the style, tempo and mood that the composer envisaged. The version here includes the chirpy opening theme, a related second theme in A minor, and the first variation on the A major theme. The full movement includes further variations on both themes.

A *leggiero* touch is essential in order to convey graceful effervescence and élan in this lovely piece, and especially in the variation. The demisemiquavers here require a soft wrist with some rotation, and nimble fingers; the notes lie well under the hand and can be executed easily provided there is no tension. Some of the LH chord transitions are a little awkward, and care is needed to ensure precision here. In the A minor section, the first semiquaver in each LH group can be held for the whole beat in accordance with eighteenth-century performance practice, creating a 'finger pedalling'.

The broad dynamics of *p* for the opening theme and *f* for the contrasting A minor section provide a starting point from which more detailed dynamics might be developed, adding shape to phrasing and the overall performance. In the A major variation that follows from bar 33, emphasizing the added syncopations (for example, in bars 43 and 49–50) will highlight Haydn's quirky sense of humour. Keeping the soft dynamic and adding a ritenuto in the final two bars will add a sense of completeness to the ending.

[A:3] **J. B. Loeillet** Minuetto (AE)

Jean Baptiste Loeillet's music embodies the growing cosmopolitanism of his time. Born in Ghent, he initially developed his career in France before moving to London around 1705, where he became a celebrated flautist, harpsichord player and teacher. Along with his younger contemporary Handel, he helped popularize the Italian style in England, introducing the music of Corelli to London audiences. His own Six Suites for harpsichord were published in 1723, and include a profusion of dance movements in popular English forms alongside the expected continental standards.

This Mineutto is characterized by simple imitation between the two hands, and maintaining an even balance is important. Secure fingering must be established in each hand, and separate practice will undoubtedly prove beneficial here, also paying attention to articulation and phrasing. Ornaments are plentiful, and need to be played nimbly on the beat, without too much emphasis. Lower mordents start on the main note, while the more occasional mordents start on the upper note.

The minuetto was a French dance in triple time, taken at a moderate pace, but Loeillet here delivers a more Italianate alternative, with a lively rhythm and lots of semiquaver movement. These should be played evenly, without *notes inégales*, and generally legato. Leaning on the first note of each bar will preserve the qualities of the dance, and at important cadence points this can become an agogic accent. At the same time, the implied accents on the second beat, for example in bar 1, should be noted; they need to be elegantly applied, and with lightness of touch.

[A:4] **W. F. Bach** Allegro in A (AE)

Wilhelm Friedemann Bach (to whom this piece is attributed) was the eldest of the four sons of J. S. Bach to enjoy a successful composing career in the mid-eighteenth century, bridging the transition from Baroque to Classical style. He wrote much for the keyboard, and his musical style is representative of the sensitive and expressive 'Empfindsamkeit' style popular in Germany at the time. In keeping with this trend, the minor-key middle section of this Allegro adds considerable drama.

The patterns of the editorial fingering suggested lie nicely under the fingers, but some passages may surprise at first, particularly the sequence of modulations from the upbeat to bars 29–32. Time devoted to slow, careful practice, hands separately, will undoubtedly be rewarded. The ornaments in bars 7 and 20 should be played as tidily and quickly as possible, with the emphasis on the main, not the grace, note.

There may be the temptation to start too fast and rush through the first section before slowing down noticeably for the more difficult minor section. Metronome practice will help establish a satisfactory tempo – ♩ = c.88 is a suggestion only. The dynamics, again editorial, give the movement a good shape, but students can feel free to try alternatives. In keeping with the Classical style, the *ff* in bars 30–32 is not a forced sound. While the given articulation offers a good guide, other approaches may be taken. But whatever interpretation is chosen, the aim is to communicate it effectively and with the confidence that the piece demands!

A:5 Handel Aria in G   (AE)

In his lifetime Handel enjoyed considerable fame as a keyboard player in addition to being a fêted composer. In a celebrated contest against Italian virtuoso Domenico Scarlatti, Handel is said to have prevailed on the organ, Scarlatti on the harpsichord. Keyboard works do not dominate Handel's output quite as they do Scarlatti's, but in his vast output there are many fine harpsichord pieces, and this ever-popular Aria in G is representative of his sparkling melodic style.

Success depends on clean fingerwork in both hands, with an even touch and rhythm. Suggested fingerings are editorial, and those whose finger dexterity allows may prefer to try fingers 5454 for the trill in the first bar, and similar thereafter. In bars 13–14 the octave jumps to the fourth finger could prove awkward for some, and finger 5 may be preferable. Unlike in J. S. Bach's more contrapuntal Inventions, Handel's two-part writing here contrasts a vigorous RH melody with a LH accompaniment, similar to a continuo part, with occasional added harmony notes. The LH can play lightly detached throughout, gently leaning on each downbeat.

The opening three-semiquaver anacrusis has a decisive impact on the rhythm throughout, and any scheme of articulation used is recommended to reflect this. The tempo indication Presto need not be taken too literally, provided that the articulation gives the piece bounce. While there are no dynamic indications, dynamics can be used to shape phrases, and the second half (from bar 9) might begin with a softer overall dynamic to add contrast. While momentum needs to be maintained to the end, a minimal ritardando might be made in the last bar.

A:6 **Kuhlau** Allegretto grazioso (AE)

Friedrich Kuhlau was a younger contemporary of Beethoven. German-born, he fled to Copenhagen following Napoleon's annexation of Hamburg in 1810. Many of his works were destroyed in 1831 when fire ripped through his apartment building. Surviving works include many charming piano and flute pieces, but best known are his popular Sonatinas, which provide ideal pedagogic preparation for the demands of Beethoven's piano works. Kuhlau's Sonatina, Op. 55, of which this piece is the finale, was published in 1823, a quarter of a century after Clementi's famous Sonatinas, Op. 36, but it has a similar musical language.

Many of the note patterns in this piece will be familiar to students from learning scales, but it might prove a challenge to play the piece with a consistent lightness of touch. Particular care is needed in the central A minor section, where the LH semiquavers (bar 58 onwards) may need slow practice to ensure evenness. LH chords must be well articulated throughout, taking care to observe the rests, and allowing the RH melody and runs to sparkle. The few ornaments are to be played as acciaccaturas, crushed notes, rather than as appoggiaturas.

The urge to play this piece too quickly must be resisted at all costs! Though some may be tempted to perform it as a dazzling showpiece, the marking Allegretto grazioso indicates the need for restraint. Dynamics must be observed with care to add colour, but without over-dramatizing the A minor middle section. An effective performance will be elegant – full of charm and poise.

B:1 **T. Kirchner** Plauderei (Chat) (FW)

This attractive Romantic miniature by German composer and pianist Theodor Kirchner shares qualities with Mendelssohn's 'Songs without Words' – a highly lyrical melody with a flowing accompaniment. The switching of the melody between the hands makes this piece a little more challenging; however, plenty of separate-hands practice will enable good balance between the melody and accompaniment to be created.

The music is marked Con moto (with movement), suggesting a feeling of forward propulsion, though the tempo should not be too fast. Students should aim for a singing legato in the melody with delicate semiquavers in the accompaniment (watching the timing to ensure the semiquaver figures come in on time). It may be easier to practise the accompaniment as a series of block chords so that the different harmonies can be heard, and a sense of the changing harmonic colours will also help shape the dynamics and mood of the piece (e.g. in bars 7–8).

 Listening to Mendelssohn's 'Songs without Words' will give the player a good sense of the character of this music, which is deeply Romantic in style. There is much scope for expressive playing, including a beautifully lyrical melodic line and the use of tempo rubato to shape the phrases and create drama, particularly in the middle section. The *rit.* in bar 11 emphasizes the suspended harmony, so any temptation to hurry through here should be avoided – perhaps by imagining an operatic soprano lingering on that high F. This makes the final bar, with its delicate arpeggiated chords, all the more delightful.

B:2 **Farrenc** Étude in A minor   (FW)

Robert Schumann praised the piano works of French pianist and composer Louise Farrenc, describing them as 'so finished – that one must fall under their charm, especially since a subtle aroma of romanticism hovers over them', and this moody little Étude demonstrates these attributes very clearly. In just 31 bars of music, Farrenc creates a striking and attractive piano miniature. This is an étude very much in the spirit of Chopin's wonderful Études, but composed to offer technical and artistic challenges to the more intermediate pianist.

This rather melancholy piece imitates the siciliana, a slowish pastoral dance in compound time with lilting dotted rhythms. It has an ABA[1] structure, and the return of the A section at bar 19 is distinguished by a more florid LH accompaniment. While this may look daunting, the LH is in fact merely broken chords that are quite straightforward; most of them are in a comfortable five-finger position. From bar 16 the semiquavers should be light and fluent. Wrist flexibility and lateral arm movement will assist the larger stretches in bars 23–5.

Students should aim for a sweet singing sound in the melody with soft accompanying chords. In bars 9–12, the top line of the melody in 3rds needs to be brought out, ensuring that all the ornaments (best played on the beat) are delicate and unforced. The changing harmonies colour the shifting moods, enhanced by subtle dynamics that shape the phrases, all of which provide scope for expressive playing.

B:3 **Sibelius** Joueur de harpe (The Harp Player)

This attractive miniature comes from Sibelius's set of ten Bagatelles, Op. 34, and is unashamedly romantic. In it the composer imitates both the articulation and sound of the harp to create a piece rich in expression, yet with a simplicity that makes it immediately appealing.

Despite the key of B flat minor, the music lies comfortably under the hands, and the main technical challenge is in articulating semiquaver arpeggios in the lento sections to suggest the sound of a strummed and plucked harp. The semiquavers should be very even, so that each note is heard, but with a rippling upward movement. The top note of each group may be played with the left hand, which will bring appropriate emphasis to create a brighter, more 'plucked' sound. Bars 17 and 18 should be played without the pedal, thus creating a drier sound in the semiquavers, though the sustained accented notes provide resonance.

Encourage your student to find a slightly different articulation for the arpeggiated chords in bars 12 and 16 to provide contrast. The Stretto sections feel improvisatory. Again, the triplet quavers should be even, the phrases shaped as indicated by the dynamics. The LH chords at the opening should move smoothly, without the pedal. An alternative suggested fingering scheme might be 1/5, 1/4, 1/4-5, 1/4, 1/5-4, 1/5, with the thumb sliding between the top notes.

The improvisatory character of the music is indicated by the changes in tempo and pauses (e.g. at bars 3 and 12). There is much scope for expression even within such a short piece: listening to romantic music for harp will inform the appropriate approach and sound.

B:4 **Bloch** Dream

Ernest Bloch (1880–1959) was born in Geneva and emigrated to America in 1916. His compositional style shows the influence of many post-Romantic composers, including Mahler, Debussy and Richard Strauss, and combines neoclassical and Jewish elements. *Enfantines* was written in 1923, and like Schumann's *Album for the Young*, the pieces have evocative titles and each is a miniature of expression combined with pedagogical purpose. Composed for Bloch's daughters to use in their piano studies, the pieces are mostly Romantic in style though the use of modes gives them a distinctly twentieth-century flavour.

'Dream' is an impressionistic tone poem in G Dorian – its key signature one of two flats but with the 6th raised to become E♮. It is technically relatively straightforward, but refined legato playing is required for both hands to create a smooth, fluid sound. The melody is accompanied by a series of broken triads in quavers. These should feel flowing and unforced: lateral wrist movement will help achieve an appropriate tone and balance of sound. Using the pedal sensitively and sparingly throughout will add atmosphere. At bar 31 the pedal can sustain the lower bass chord while the LH hand travels up the register. In bars 32, 34 and 35 the LH crosses over the RH to play the high D dotted crotchet. Marked staccato, this should have a distinct 'ping' to contrast with the lower notes in the LH and the RH quavers.

Although this atmospheric piece is confined to a restrained dynamic range, it offers plenty of scope for expression, including clear shaping of the melody, subtle highlighting of the changes of harmony in the accompaniment, and the use of tempo rubato.

B:5 | **Franck** Poco lento

César Franck (1822–90) was born in Liège, in present-day Belgium, and despite winning prizes for his compositions while at the Paris Conservatory, he did not gain public recognition for his music until later in his life. He was better known as an organist, and one can readily imagine this serious and expressive prelude being played on the organ. It comes from a collection of pieces for harmonium (a type of small organ) and translates well to the piano where its harmonic originality can truly be appreciated.

A simple RH melody is accompanied by piquant bass chords, and much of the melancholy character of the piece comes from the LH. In bars 8, 10 and 12, for the hairpins (referring to the accompaniment) students can use a 'swell' of sound to highlight this movement in the LH notes; the chords are taken by the RH, except in bar 12, where the LH plays all three notes. The LH throughout contains many leaps of an octave or more, and practice might include moving from a chord's preceding note to the chord's lowest note, its middle note and its top note, and finally the chord in its entirety, using the same fingering each time. Separate-hands practice will also ensure that both LH and RH parts are well known.

The RH is straightforward, but despite its simplicity there is much scope for expression, and students should aim for a smooth cantabile with some tonal rise and fall within each phrase. The character of the piece is generally slow and serious, while the chromaticism adds a bittersweet atmosphere to the music.

B:6 | **Schumann** Erinnerung (In Memory)

Robert Schumann's *Album for the Young* is that rare thing in piano literature: a suite of pieces that combine artistry and expression with pedagogical demands, and his beautiful miniatures remain among the best-loved music for piano. The pieces are based on poetic ideas, as evidenced by some of their titles, and Schumann's primary concern was to encourage expressive play-ing. Written in memory of Felix Mendelssohn (the date of his death appears underneath the title) and composed in the style of one of his lyrical 'songs without words', this piece is ideal for the more musically sensitive student with a well-developed technique.

The main technical issues are coordination, tone and balance. The RH mel-ody requires careful control of weight and tone to give it a singing quality

– not always an easy task when the hand has to play chords as well. Finger changes and a good sense of connection to the keys will be necessary to achieve a very smooth legato line, and playing or singing only the top line's notes will help your student to hear the melody clearly. The LH part will benefit from secure, well-learnt fingering, wrist flexibility and a mobile fore-arm to help the hand travel through the notes. At the end of each semiquaver run a springing-off the final note will create a little propulsion to move to the quaver that follows.

Although scored in A major, the music has a distinctly bittersweet quality, achieved through colourful harmonies, tempo rubato (some of it marked, some implied – e.g. bars 9–10) and fermatas. *Nicht schnell* means 'not fast', and a calmly flowing andante will achieve the appropriate tempo and atmos-phere for this music.

C:1 Lutosławski Rektor (The Schoolmaster)

The Polish composer Witold Lutosławski produced some excellent music for developing pianists. 'Rektor' comes from a collection of 12 folk melodies and shows the composer at his most direct, rhythmically incisive and energized.

This piece will do wonders for technical development if practised consist-ently and with the awareness that patience is needed early on! Students should do all they can to cultivate a reliable and comfortable staccato tech-nique in both hands. Practising staccato scales and five-finger exercises will be good preparatory work here. In the early stages it is worth breaking the piece down: practising up to speed but at a quiet dynamic level in small units (a bar or two at a time), and ensuring that fingering is consistent and secure, will avoid stiffness and tension in the wrists. As confidence increases it will be possible to play up to speed at the written dynamic level and for longer stretches at a time.

The percussive style and sparse textures mean that very little pedalling is required. Taking special care over the projection of articulation will give per-sonality to the interpretation. In particular the RH second-beat accents beginning in bar 4 could be given special character if the wrist is lifted imme-diately before the accents are played, though it is important not to delay notes as this will lead to rhythmic distortion. Indeed the motoric character of this music means that a clear pulse is necessary throughout. A clear sense of metre needs to be kept in bars 31–4, and the change of gear to Vivace (bar 53) should be communicated confidently and at a consistent speed.

C:2 Prokofiev Lentamente

Sergey Prokofiev is one of the most important composers of twentieth-century piano music and his *Visions fugitives* (Fleeting Visions), Op. 22, are well established in the repertoire. The 20 miniatures are highly varied in mood and were completed in 1917 as the composer fled from communist Russia. This opening number of the set has a quiet, dream-like characterization.

Cultivating a reliable legato-pedal technique will be invaluable here. Each melody note might be pedalled separately. Using arm weight for the RH melody and ensuring that the LH is played in a lighter manner will create the appropriate balance. In the RH of bars 14–20, slow practice could help with coordination, with weight added to the melody while playing the quavers more *leggiero*. There should be no break in the phrasing of the top line over bars 17–18.

It may be helpful for students to 'orchestrate' this piece in their inner ear. The RH melody seems evocative of a solo flute, though some may prefer to imagine it realized by violins. Even though the dynamic level is hushed, this melodic line needs to be projected convincingly over the rest of the texture, and to reflect the different markings on the text: a clear differentiation between *p*, *pp* and *ppp* will ensure greater characterization. Ubiquitous use of the *una corda* pedal should be avoided, and reserving it for the drops to *ppp* (bars 9, 15 and 22) will enable more tonal variety.

C:3 Mike Cornick Film Noir

Mike Cornick's special talent for using popular idioms attractively within the remits of educational piano music has been widely recognized by exam boards, and his music has proved to be especially popular with teenage pianists. He writes music that is extremely idiomatic for piano but which, perhaps paradoxically, often evokes extra-pianistic connotations!

This is an excellent vehicle for developing variety of touch and voicing of chords. The RH chords from bar 1 will be more lugubrious if the lowest note is given extra weight – playing each chord but releasing the upper two notes while holding onto the lowest. In the LH an effective double-bass pizzicato from bar 17 can be achieved if fingers are placed over notes in advance, then quickly released. The RH 3rds in bars 9 and 11 can be realized effectively with arm movements. Using an overlapping technique will make them feel more secure and reliable. Indeed, for much of this piece a 'physical legato' – holding RH notes on for longer than their written value – could prove an invaluable approach.

This music requires a strong rhythmic awareness and control. Spending time clapping and humming each part away from the instrument will be useful not only early on but also throughout the learning process: bad rhythmic habits can easily slip into a piece in a popular idiom when it has been under the fingers for a few months or more. The aim should be precision rather than

approximation. Students should enjoy the sense of musical space and cele-
brate the delicious harmonies, using the sustaining pedal as a tonal agent to
add reverberation and 'glow' at the end of long notes.

[C:4] **Gillock** New Orleans Nightfall

This has been a particularly popular piece with younger pianists over the
years. It immediately establishes a strong, memorable characterization of the
blues, and includes an excitingly energized faster middle section that is fun to
play. While the music offers many opportunities to explore characterization
and contrasts of colour, it always remains well within the confines of idiomatic, comfortable writing for the instrument.

Strong rhythms are essential in bars 13–20. Clapping them regularly, even
when the piece is very familiar, will reinforce authority and control. The
accented chords near the ends of bars 14, 16 and 18 can be executed with
wrist staccato, and sharp and fast flicking upward movements away from the
piano towards the body will be effective. Pedal changes at the ends of bars in
the outer sections are to be clear and confident, and in these outer sections
highlighting the contrasting textures will be important and should be developed with careful aural awareness. Exaggerating the RH melody line by practising it *f* or even *ff* while playing the bass-clef notes *p* will help to instil a
sense of melodic projection. Recording the piece, then listening back and
checking how effectively the tonal differences between melody and chordal
accompaniment are conveyed, is an exercise that will reap rewards.

This piece strongly evokes colours and sonorities of non-keyboard instruments. It is easy to imagine the world of New Orleans jazz – as well as the
score of Gershwin's *An American in Paris* – when beginning to play the
deliciously sensuous, dreamy opening. Going through the entire piece and
'orchestrating' it could prove to be another highly effective and inspiring
exercise.

[C:5] **Poulenc** Valse Tyrolienne

The French composer-pianist Francis Poulenc (1899–1963) was a prolific
piano miniaturist. The effervescence, joy and energy of many of his ever-
fresh works for the instrument pervade this popular *morceau*.

The need for ease and confidence in using the pedal with a consistent LH
waltz rhythm would make a good starting point for practice. An aim would be
to clear the pedal for each bar's third beat, making sure that the pedal action
is not overly heavy and accented. Avoiding looking down at the LH as it leaps
from the single first-beat notes to the higher second and third beats will
ensure the best tonal effect. Meanwhile the deliciously banal RH melody
requires strong and commanding projection. It might inspire and be helpful

to experiment by playing it first an octave higher than written, then to try and emulate that higher register's greater brilliance and sparkle in the note range given on the score.

Unadulterated optimism and confidence are important to project in music that speaks with candour and immediacy. There will be no need to use rubato for expressive purposes – on the contrary, it is vital not to deviate from a steady pulse, and the humour and wit of this send-up of a traditional Austrian waltz will be lost if a regular beat isn't sustained. In order that the wit and variety of colour comes across, staccatos and accents (first seen in bars 3 and 4) should be distinguished clearly. The slurred crotchet, four quaver figures also add character to the piece and can be realized as one continuous sweeping gesture: being too aware of the notes as individual crotchets and quavers risks making them overly ponderous.

C:6   Pam Wedgwood   Hang-Up

Pam Wedgwood's special talent for writing in a wide range of popular styles for the needs of less experienced pianists embraces not only a deep knowledge of compositional craftsmanship but also an idiomatic understanding of the instrument. Here she embraces the Latin American rhythmic style with characteristic flair and an arresting range of pianistic devices.

The main technical priority in this excitingly syncopated number is strong, sustained rhythmic conviction. In terms of pianism, it is important to avoid blocked wrists while playing the repeated triads in bar 1. Loose wrists are also important for the shifts in position in bars 5, 8 and elsewhere: indeed, the piece can be viewed as a study for controlled wrist relaxation. While it will help to keep close to the keys to realize articulation with control and accuracy, it is perhaps even more important to establish and maintain freedom of movement throughout. Students with smaller hands may need to deploy extra flexibility in the LH elbow to safely navigate the intervals spanning a 9th or 10th in, for example, bars 5 and 6: pivoting on the second (quaver) note of each bar, allowing the elbow to move, will enable the playing to become effortless.

This music has a delightful simplicity, with a natural ease and sense of flow to it. In performance it will be important that the very specifically marked tempo and dynamic markings are not made to sound artificial or contrived: the many contrasts, rather than being 'implanted' onto the interpretation, need to seem inevitable! Students can enjoy the dance-like energy – and let the music speak for itself.

GRADE 6

A:1 **T. A. Arne** Andante

Thomas Augustine Arne, one of the most distinguished English composers of the Baroque era, wrote sonata movements for keyboard inspired by dance forms, as well as toccatas and more simple airs. Arne's keyboard music often shows the influence of Scarlatti and Handel, which can be immediately heard in this charming Andante, with its rhythmic impetus and florid melodic line.

Practising this movement without the trills at first is advisable, ensuring that all the essential notes and rhythms are firmly in place. Working on the trills in isolation would come next – building them up from slow speeds, and keeping fingers close to the keys. Knowing exactly how many notes are played in each trill will help enormously. It might also be beneficial to practise all the trills in triplets, keeping a legato approach consistently in place.

Rhythmically this music will benefit from a sense of impetus on its first and third beats. The metre needs to be well-defined: the opening quaver upbeat can move the music forward with character and so should not be laboured. As with all Baroque music there are many articulation possibilities. Using a consistently detached touch for all of the quavers could be appropriate. The triplet semiquavers from bar 3 onwards might be thought of in terms of bowing, either as two-note slurs followed by staccato single semiquavers, or in groups of six legato notes at a time. Stylistically this music is evocative of an aria from Italian opera – so trying to sing the RH part while playing the LH may be a useful exercise.

A:2 **J. S. Bach** Fugue in G

J. S. Bach's magnificent keyboard works can be arranged in a 'ladder of learning', with the Two- then the Three-Part Inventions leading directly to the early Preludes and Fughettas, then to the all-encompassing 48 Preludes and Fugues (*The Well-Tempered Clavier*). This G major Fugue was later substantially revised, so comparing the two versions of this work offers a glimpse into the extraordinary compositional workings of Bach's musical mind.

The Fughetta is easier to master if a generic legato is avoided. It will therefore help, in advance of studying the score, to develop a facility with broken-chord, scale and arpeggio figurations hands separately and together, using staccato and semi-legato articulation. Work on the piece itself can then begin at a slow tempo and at a dynamic level of *p*, subsequently increasing the tempo gradually, always ensuring that comfort and ease are in place. The triads in bars 53–8 may be managed effectively if the lower two notes are consistently released while the upper notes alone are bound together with overlapping legato.

The dance-like characterization will be emphasized if the piece is felt as one-in-a-bar rather than three. Dynamics are left to the player's discretion, but one option might be to highlight modulations with a change in dynamic. Crescendos to phrase peaks as well as diminuendos afterwards can be effective too – for example, starting p at bar 27 before a gradual crescendo through to the high point at bar 40, then a diminuendo through to the move to B minor (bar 45). The characterization is optimistic and positive in this fugue, so a stable and comfortable pulse will be welcome throughout.

A:3 J. L. Dussek Allegro

The keyboard compositions of Jan Ladislav Dussek hold a pivotal role in the history of music. He wrote around 42 sonatas, which influenced Beethoven and anticipated much of what followed in the early Romantic era – in terms of not only some motifs and chromatic harmonies, but also textures and the need to use the sustaining pedal in particular passages.

A comfortable, economical LH rotary technique will facilitate the extensive LH Alberti-bass figurations. This involves pivoting on the fifth-finger notes, releasing any tension in the wrist and allowing the other fingers a light touch while the wrist remains loose – practising single beats and stopping, then half and finally whole bars at a stretch, gradually increasing the tempo of each small musical unit. RH 6ths and 3rds will work well with relaxed arm movements. The 3rds in bars 23–8 can sparkle if each hand position is prepared in advance, resting fingers on the keys before releasing each 3rd with energized finger movements towards the body.

The RH semiquavers can sound convincing if realized as a mixture of staccato and slurred groups. Indeed, using both *leggiero* and staccato touches is preferable to a generic legato throughout. Excitement can be created within an appropriate stylistic context if the LH chords are arpeggiated quickly (e.g. in bars 6 and 8). Overuse of the pedal could blur textures, but short 'dabs' for the quavers in the opening bar, for example, may add welcome resonance to a still, clear texture. Elsewhere 'finger pedalling' may be an appropriate alternative to footwork, and some of the Alberti-bass figurations can easily afford this approach – the lowest notes (fifth finger) sustaining and overlapping with the other semiquavers in each beat.

A:4 J. S. Bach Menuet 1 and Menuet 2

J. S. Bach's Six Partitas are cornerstone works of the concert repertoire. The first Partita, BWV 825, is one of the most popular choices for student and professional players alike. It is easy to see why: its melodic memorability and optimistic characterization are harnessed to Baroque dance rhythms that seem to leap off the page.

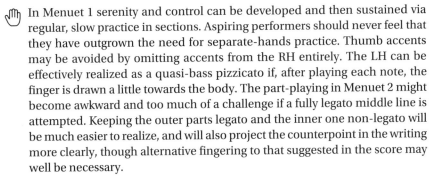

In Menuet 1 serenity and control can be developed and then sustained via regular, slow practice in sections. Aspiring performers should never feel that they have outgrown the need for separate-hands practice. Thumb accents may be avoided by omitting accents from the RH entirely. The LH can be effectively realized as a quasi-bass pizzicato if, after playing each note, the finger is drawn a little towards the body. The part-playing in Menuet 2 might become awkward and too much of a challenge if a fully legato middle line is attempted. Keeping the outer parts legato and the inner one non-legato will be much easier to realize, and will also project the counterpoint in the writing more clearly, though alternative fingering to that suggested in the score may well be necessary.

This music can come alive if it is infused with rhythmic buoyancy and character from the first to the last bars. Playing Menuet 2 at the same tempo as Menuet 1 works well, but it is not essential for success and a slower tempo may be adopted if desired. Imagining the quavers of Menuet 1 as a violinist might bow them could prove useful, as would considering where a vocalist would take breaths. Relating the music to singing can instil confidence and conviction as well as enhance the shaping of the phrases themselves.

A:5 | Cimarosa Sonata No. 17

The Italian Domenico Cimarosa (1749–1801) has left a prolific legacy of keyboard sonatas, which are surprisingly neglected. Much of his music is characterful and convincing within a Classical, often operatic, context. This elegant, poised and expressive movement is notable for its deployment of 3rds and 6ths.

Flowing movements and controlled legato in the upper melody part especially should be prioritized. The lower notes in the RH in bars 1–7 may be practised and played non-legato. Using fingering that connects the notes of the RH's upper part but allows its lower part to remain non-legato will enable the top line to 'sing' more expressively, projecting with greater ease over the rest of the texture. A similar approach can be used for the LH in bars 26–8. Playing the staccato quavers in bars 13–15 with too short an attack risks losing their inherent poetry and melodic charm; they need to be sonorous, and played with wrists and elbows that are relaxed. Using arm weight can give them more sonority and richness.

An awareness of Classical style should be balanced with a sense of poetry, cantabile and expansive expression. Regarding the deployment of the pedal, it may be useful to start from the premiss that 'less is more'. There should be no reason to use the *una corda* in this piece, even though inexperienced pianists may wish to obtain a sense of technical control by doing so. There is little need either for the use of the sustaining pedal, though as a means of connecting repeated notes in the RH it could prove useful – if executed with tasteful discretion.

A:6 **Kuhlau** Rondo: Vivace

🧩 The German composer Friedrich Kuhlau (1786–1832) has provided us with a wealth of material that is not only well-crafted and of great educational value, but often charming and characterful as well. This highly energized dance-like movement is notable for its filigree RH passagework and optimistic characterization.

🖐 The challenging RH part can be practised in small sections, isolating and so giving full attention to each technical issue. These might be sections as small as a single bar, and even smaller musical units within that. The opening bars are a good example: RH bars 1–2 may confuse simply because the suggested fingering (which may be used throughout the piece) is not one that is conventionally used for a G major scale! Working at the second and third notes of bar 3 alone, becoming familiar with the thumb moving under finger 2, will be time well spent, as it is so often position shifts that cause insecurity and uncertainty in performance. Similarly, when semiquavers appear in the LH (bars 39 and 107), practising the apparently simple thumb manoeuvre from B to G on its own will be worthwhile.

🎨 A strong and consistent rhythmic pulse is essential throughout in order to maintain continuity, and students should avoid starting this movement at a speed that has to be compromised later. There is a danger of accompanimental textures becoming too heavy, especially as the RH semiquavers need to be *leggiero* and mostly at *p* rather than *f*. It may be helpful to use as little pedal as possible: the indication for the held first-beat notes in the LH implies a 'finger-pedal' approach, one in which it is helpful to overlap and connect notes with the fingers themselves.

B:1 **Bruch** Moderato

🧩 The German composer Max Bruch is remembered mostly for his first Violin Concerto with its extremely beautiful slow movement. This intensely passionate and lyrical piano miniature was composed when Bruch was in his early 20s and it typifies his Romantic style, similar to that of his compatriot Johannes Brahms.

🖐 The piece displays much pianistic flair and rich harmonization together with a wealth of expression. The mood of the music is dark and intense and players will need to have sensitive control of the tone and dynamics to achieve an authentic character, with the position of the slurs being carefully noted. The

LH accompaniment remains largely the same throughout the piece. Careful practising to position the jump between the lower note and the chord accurately is essential. A light staccato is appropriate in the LH – bearing in mind that this music will be pedalled and that the distinct articulation of the LH notes should not be blurred by too much pedal. The *una corda* pedal might be used for the bars marked *pp* to create an even softer, more veiled sound. The octaves in bars 10 and 38 should be approached with a relaxed hand.

The melody is quite repetitive and much of the interest in this music comes from the changes in dynamics and the LH harmonies. There is much scope for expression, however, and phrases can be shaped with both dynamics and tempo rubato to reflect their contours and the climactic moments in the music, for example at bars 9–12. Student and teacher can explore the characteristics of different intervals and experiment using agogic accents (e.g. in bar 31) and rubato to create greater dramatic effect.

[B:2] **Chopin** Prelude in B minor

Chopin's 24 Preludes, Op. 28, one in each of the major and minor keys, are among his best-loved piano miniatures. They present a microcosm of all the distinctive features of his music, each conveying a specific idea or emotion, and remain hugely popular with pianists and audiences. The Prelude in B minor was played at Chopin's funeral and its melancholy melody slowly unfolds in the LH.

The primary challenge, technically and also artistically, is shaping the arpeggiated LH melody against the sobbing quavers in the RH. Balance between the hands is crucial, as the RH acts as the accompaniment, and this can be achieved with plenty of separate-hands practice. The LH melody should be approached with the smoothness and resonance of a cello line (the Étude in C sharp minor, Op. 25 No. 7, offers useful further listening as it is organized in the same way). Settling on a secure fingering scheme combined with wrist flexibility in the LH semiquavers will help achieve a smooth legato line.

The music offers much scope for expressive playing and students should not hold back in emphasizing the mournful mood. As well as observing the dynamic markings, it is important to be aware of the climaxes and anti-climaxes as high and low points in the music in terms of dynamic colour, expression and breathing space within the phrases. (Bars 12 and 18 are an example of each.) Sensitive pedalling will ensure that the melody line is not obscured and that the RH quavers are clear but not overpowering.

[B:3] **Schubert** Scherzo in B flat

This, the first of Schubert's Two Scherzos for piano, is in Scherzo and Trio (ternary) form and is immediately appealing with its humorous character, sprightly rhythms and a lovely contrasting trio in E flat major. Previously integral to the structure of the Classical era piano sonata, the scherzo, in Schubert's hands, became an independent piano piece in its own right, an approach that was later taken up by Chopin, among others.

Much of the character of the A section comes from the recurring rocking trip-let figure, the subtle differences in articulation (for example, staccato within a slur which requires a different touch to unslurred staccato notes), a fer-mata, and the rests, which should be given their full value. The short grace notes (bars 2, 3, 6, 7, and so on) should be played on the beat, lightly and rapidly with a slight 'bite' to highlight the dissonance created with the follow-ing quaver. The triplets in bars 28–33 will benefit from a flexible wrist and some lateral arm movement. The contrasting Trio is warm in mood, the sprightly rhythms of the opening section replaced by longer legato phrases and sonorities that suggest lower strings and woodwind. Secure fingering in both RH and LH will ensure that bars 67–72 can be played with the requisite smoothness. In this passage care also needs to be taken over the different slur markings between the hands. The turns should feel unhurried and elegant, the RH melody underpinned by the dotted minims in the LH and upper voice. Throughout the piece the pedal should be used for musical colour rather than purely to assist legato playing.

This piece contains many distinctive elements of Schubert's writing includ-ing the use of rests and pauses to create drama and breathing spaces, and rapid shifts of mood, indicated by dynamic contrasts. Close attention to these details will result in a performance that is authentic and characterful.

B:4 Grovlez Petites litanies de Jésus (Little litanies to Jesus) (FW)

Gabriel Grovlez was taught by Fauré and was a contemporary of Debussy, and there are echoes of both composers in this beautiful miniature, from the naive, tender melody to the distinctly twentieth-century harmonies. The music often moves homophonically, suggesting sacred choral music of the period. In 'Petites litanies de Jésus' the rhythm of Tristan Klingsor's poem scans with the charming melody of this piece. Each verse closes with the words 'Souriez-moi' (Smile on me), which fit perfectly with the music in bars 5–6 and 33–4, and the final chord in these bars must be held for its full value to reflect the music's title and achieve a beatific quality.

A comfortable octave stretch is needed for several of the chords, as these should not be arpeggiated and should be carefully voiced. Good fingering for all the chords (e.g. 4/1, 5/2, 4/1, 5/3 in the RH of bar 1) combined with wrist flexibility will enable the student to play the melody line legato and with a clear cantabile tone (like that of a chorister's voice). Some finger changing may be necessary in places such as bar 5 of the RH (here, finger 4 changing to 5 on the second beat) in order to achieve a smooth effect. Sensitive pedalling will sustain a smooth legato and lend resonance to the sound without losing clarity in the melody line. (It can be assumed that the *una corda* indication applies to bar 27 and the first two beats of bar 28 only.)

 Supple phrasing with dynamic contours and some broadening of tempo at the end of each phrase will bring shape and expression to the music, and reflect the poem's cadences, while also communicating the simplicity and reverent mood of the piece.

B:5 C. Hartmann The Little Ballerina (FW)

🎹 The Norwegian composer Christian Hartmann (1910–85) wrote many fine pieces, and his song settings for Ole Brumm (Winnie-the-Pooh) are familiar to all Norwegian children. This dainty waltz, composed for his son's niece when she was five years old, evokes a graceful ballet dancer pirouetting on her pointes.

🖐 Though technically fairly straightforward, the piece includes a few unexpected twists, such as the LH jump from bass to treble register in bar 10, but the composer has helpfully written a *rit.* here to make this jump less perilous and to encourage players to take their time. The RH part offers excellent opportunities to gain confidence in reading high notes on leger lines. Good fingering and wrist flexibility will ensure the RH quavers flow smoothly. The first two bars act as an introduction – one can imagine the ballerina preparing to begin her performance – and a little broadening of tempo in bar 2 will create a sense of expectation. Although the music is scored in one-bar phrases, students can be encouraged to think in longer phrases (e.g. bars 3–10, then 11–18), subdivided into phraselets, and to shape the music accordingly. The ornaments should be light and delicate and come just before the beat.

 The music owes something to the beautiful, elegant waltzes of Chopin and Brahms, and some further listening – such as to Chopin's Op. 70 Nos. 1 and 3 – will inspire plenty of ideas about musical shape, tempo (including tempo rubato) and dynamic shading for character and expression. The LH accompaniment should be clear but not too 'oom-pah-pah'. The pedal is best used only sparingly throughout: the RH part is so very pretty that too much pedal may obscure the delicacy of the melody.

B:6 Rebikov Feuille d'automne (Autumn Leaf) (FW)

🎹 The music of Vladimir Rebikov (1866–1920) is now largely neglected, and he is mostly remembered today for his salon music and piano miniatures. This atmospheric piece, lamenting the turning of the year, is a charming example and owes something to 'October' from Tchaikovsky's *The Seasons*, with its intimate lyricism and bittersweet mood. A simple RH melody is enhanced by piquant harmonies and a sorrowful 'sighing' motif in the LH.

The primary challenge is shaping the melody, which will really benefit from elegant legato and a cantabile tone. The triplets should be kept in time, particularly where they are set over LH duplets. Highlighting the sighing motif in the LH will increase the sorrowful mood of the piece. Other LH details, such as the quavers in bars 17–18 and 25, can also be brought out to add contrast to the melodic line. The pedal will enhance the atmosphere further. The coda begins at bar 44 with an additional RH voice of descending crotchets. A distinctively different sound can be sought for this additional voice, to contrast with the drop slurs (also in the RH).

While the mood and atmosphere is subdued and melancholy, there is much scope for expressive playing and the phrases lend themselves to sensitive dynamic shaping. Each time the RH melody appears, a slightly different musical colour within the stated dynamic range will intensify the emotion of the piece. There are opportunities, too, for the use of rubato, in order to create breathing space between phrases. The final bars are especially poignant, the RH triplets spooling upwards with a light wash of pedal.

C:1 **Darius Brubeck** Tugela Rail (FL)

This laid-back jazz piano solo is a wonderful treat for students looking for a change of genre within the Grade 6 syllabus. The pianist's LH acts as rhythm and bass and keeps strict time under the improvisatory melody of the RH, as it takes us on a train journey through the countryside of KwaZulu-Natal. The repetitive rhythm of the train travelling over the tracks climaxes with the series of accented chords in bars 35–8, before the journey is resumed.

Clapping while counting quavers will help establish the strict rhythm of the LH, introduced in the first four bars of consecutive 5th chords. The main theme in the RH of parallel 6th chords sings out over this and is followed by a different, almost descant, figure at bars 13–16 as the soloist appears to improvise at a higher pitch before coming back down onto the tracks in bars 17–20 with a progression featuring unexpected offbeat accented or staccato chords. The wisps of melody interspersed between the chords, while still f, could be played with a less bold dynamic, as if woodwind rather than brass. The progression of offbeat chords beginning in bar 35, if practised slowly, counting quavers, and then played as if not being counted, will enable a fluent climax at bar 37. Legato playing of the RH chords from bar 39 can be achieved by careful and smooth fingering of the top line, listening for evenness, using the LH pedal changes to support.

The different sounds and timbres of a jazz trio can be found on Brubeck's *Tugela Rail and Other Tracks* via Spotify. The LH is drum and bass and the RH piano and saxophone soloist.

C:2   **Ibert**   Sérénade sur l'eau (Serenade on the Water)   FL

The title conjures up the image of boating down the Seine on a summer's day, as if in a Monet painting. Perhaps the sun is out, the boat is gently rocking, and someone is lazily humming as their fingers trail in the water. Ibert's ostinato LH describes the motion of the boat and the serenade is sung by the RH. This is a delightful, evocative little piece which is ideal for small hands and pianists who enjoy bringing a picture to life.

The $\frac{9}{8}$ time signature might be simply introduced using the LH ostinato and by counting 1, 2 and 3 to each quaver and crotchet. Once this is established the RH can flow gently over it. The RH has both melody and accompaniment as indicted by the *il canto sost.* direction of bar 3 and the semiquavers with stems down. A legato fingering and slightly heavier fingers will bring out the melody while lighter fingers just reaching the key bed will let the accompaniment ripple quietly along. The priority for the RH 3rds at bars 13 and 14 is to keep the top line smooth while a dextrous thumb manages the underneath notes. In the passage beginning at bar 15 the quavers should be gently pointed to indicate the direction of the melody, while the chromatic semiquavers are less important.

Legato pedalling changing on the dotted-crotchet beats will bring sophistication and help in creating legato. Judicious use of rubato might add to the feeling of being at the mercy of the water, while time spent practising a controlled *poco rall.* in the final bars, and ending with barely a ripple, will not be wasted.

C:3   **Federico Ruiz**   Un amanecer en Santa Marta   FL
(At Dawn in Santa Marta)

Ruiz is well known in South America for fusing classical and Latin American folk styles in his music, here delightfully exemplified in this gem of a dance with its infectious Latin rhythms and appealing melodies within a theme and variations structure. 'At Dawn in Santa Marta' begins quietly with the main theme and becomes gradually busier as it bustles through three variations, concluding with a lively finger-staccato variation punctuated by light LH chords.

Practising the LH first will help to ensure that it is rock steady and that the articulation and dynamics are securely established. The accompanimental style of the theme and first variation gives way to imitation in variation two (from bar 18); the RH and LH dialogue during this passage needs to be equally voiced. In the second half a light wrist staccato with LH fingers kept close to the keys will aid an even *mp* attack, while slow practice with the suggested fingering will help keep the RH fingers flowing over bar-lines to the end of each phrase. Practising the RH final variation with a quick, light finger-staccato touch, slowly and then up to tempo, will prevent any undue accents. Before playing the notes it may help to mark where the RH and LH notes coincide and slowly tap out the variation with both hands.

A sophisticated and convincing performance will not only observe the dynamics on the score but shape each phrase within the written dynamic. It will be worthwhile to spend time on the last two bars and the final leap onto an accented subito *p* chord to create an ending with impact.

C:4 R. R. Bennett Eight Maids a-Milking   FL

The British composer Richard Rodney Bennett composed piano music, operatic works and pieces for orchestra as well as music for films and TV, writing in a variety of styles including jazz. This piece, in ternary form, is taken from his collection *Partridge Pie* based on the carol 'The 12 Days of Christmas'. It presents a picture of milkmaids bustling around rounding up cows and then settling down to the calmer process of milking before dashing off again.

The irregular time signature of $\frac{7}{8}$ might cause some initial difficulty, but tapping out both hands while counting aloud each section may help here. A light finger staccato, just reaching the base of the keys, will achieve the spiky sound required for the outer sections, whereas the middle section beginning at bar 11 (written as bar 10) calls for the exact opposite – a quieter legato sound. The finger 1 and the bracket on the first quaver of bars 14, 16, and 18 (indicating that the thumb is to bridge both notes) may not be possible, in which case any alternative fingering should allow a lovely legato line to be produced. The short two-bar coda – no slowing down – is marked *f* and is heavily accented. This can be effectively achieved with more arm weight as the piece progresses towards a triumphant *sf* and *ff*.

Work will be needed to convey the complete change of character between the outer and middle sections. Often we think we are achieving such contrast in dynamics and mood but in fact are falling short. Students might therefore record their practice and listen back, or seek someone else's honest opinion, in order to build awareness and so paint this farmyard picture fully.

C:5 Michel Legrand One at a Time   FL

Michel Legrand is a French composer, conductor and jazz pianist, probably best known for his haunting, jazz-influenced film music. 'One at a Time', released in 1969, is a relaxed ballad that would belong comfortably in a jazz club, accompanied by soft brush strokes on the snare drum.

Time spent achieving rhythmic accuracy in this piece will never be wasted, especially in conveying the difference between the pairs of quavers, triplets and semiquavers, all of which appear in the first bar. Perhaps the drummer's trick of using words will help? The LH D minor chords (bar 2 and similar) may be too large for some hands so these could be spread – but ensuring that the top note arrives on beat 1. Legato pedalling will add richness and a cantabile feel but in the final bar direct pedalling on each chord will add emphasis to the *molto rall.*

The piece will benefit from a relaxed approach to the tempo – the give and take of rubato adding to the jazz-club ambience – easing off at the end of the phrase in bar 8, pushing the pace on a little during the *cresc.* from bar 19 then relaxing it again in bars 23, before easing into an *a tempo* in bar 25. This is an opportunity to be both the song and the accompaniment, so becoming familiar with the lyrics will be beneficial. Singing the words will help students decide on and define the dynamics and the rise and fall of each phrase.

C:6 Shostakovich Prelude in F sharp minor

Shostakovich's 24 Preludes, Op. 34, were composed in the winter of 1932, as the Cultural Revolution was in progress. This initiated a period of artistic repression, and composers such as Shostakovich trod a fine line between what they wanted to write and what would be officially approved. Shostakovich took inspiration not only from the preludes of Bach and of Chopin (whose preludes were also organized around the circle of 5ths), but from styles and genres of other periods. This scherzo-like No. 8 has at its heart the folk music of Russia and Ukraine.

Bringing out the separate LH and RH voices will come from slow practice hands-separately in sections. A light, crisp staccato touch with fingers close to the keys will contrast beautifully with the marked slurs, and playing the acciaccaturas exactly as written will add to the humorous effect. Shostakovich was less helpful with fingering: there is none marked! Deciding on this early on will pay dividends when playing at a faster, Allegretto pace. The articulation of the RH 5ths of bar 36 can be achieved with a down-up wrist movement for the two-note slur, then keeping the wrist high for the two semiquaver staccato notes. The trills (bars 23 and 24) might be played as four demisemiquavers per LH quaver beat, or as quickly as students can manage without disruption to a steady LH.

This prelude has a lively, unpredictable character, suggestive of the acrobatics of circus clowns. Listening to all the pieces in the set and the comparable *Dances of the Dolls* will give a feel for the style and tonality, and Shostakovich's own performance of the prelude is available on YouTube.

GRADE 7

A:1 **Handel** Gigue (FL)

Handel's great eight keyboard suites represent his most important contribution to Baroque keyboard music, and this nimble Gigue, a dance usually in compound time and with a contrapuntal texture, provides a lively finish to the final suite. It is a very attractive Baroque choice for students at this level, with its opening theme spanning one-and-a-half octaves, contrasting legato dialogues (such as in bars 6–9), and a 'giant steps' theme (bars 10–11).

Coming to a decision on a stylish articulation that can be adhered to throughout will be helped by slow separate-hands practice in short sections, listening attentively. While some may be able to manage the suggested ornament realizations, others might prefer to simplify them in order to keep the tempo consistent. Practising ornaments not once but at every octave on the piano could help with this. The LH giant steps at bars 10–11 and similar will benefit from isolated practice, and early memorizing of the RH here will enable students to concentrate on the LH. Most of the offbeat LH quavers here may be fingered 2-1 instead of the marked 1-2.

The lack of dynamics on the page provides an opportunity to take ownership of the Gigue and demonstrate musicality and understanding of the style. Its three-part texture can be illustrated with light and shade, showing a feeling for the interplay between the voices – for example, allowing the RH dotted crotchets in bars 6–9 and similar passages to sing out over the underlying semiquavers. It would be appropriate to end the first section with a *poco rall.* and perhaps a spread chord, and doing the same but in a more pronounced manner would be a stylish finish. Listening to performances of this movement on the harpsichord will give insights into its exciting and energetic character.

A:2 **Haydn** Tempo di Minuetto (FL)

This charming finale to one of Haydn's later sonatas dances with elegance and style through double 3rds, scales, arpeggios, ornaments and cross-rhythms. Completed in about 1789/90, this sonata would have been intended for the fortepiano rather than the harpsichord. The minuet proceeds in a conventional manner but the appearance of a second trio in E flat minor is unexpected and darker, almost Beethovian.

To secure the effortless onward flow needed for the main theme's cross-rhythms it will be helpful, as well as separate-hands practice and tapping and playing hands together, to 'feel' the two-against-three using words such as 'nice cup of tea'. The many turns are a delicate decoration of the melody line and need less weight than the main notes. The double 3rds will benefit from slow practice to achieve as legato a line as possible, and working in the different hand groups and using different rhythms may help to secure the fluency here. Careful listening will enable scales and arpeggios to pass from hand to hand in an unbroken stream, and where the RH melody is dominant the LH is quieter with fingers closer to the keys. The harmonies and patterns of broken-chord passages (e.g. at bars 73–84 and 103–8) will become more apparent when practised as solid chords.

The dynamics (some editorial) are a broad guide but a more expressive stylish performance will include rise and fall within these phrases and shaped feminine endings at imperfect cadences – strong to weak with a down-and-up movement of the wrist. A recognition that the student knows where each phrase is going can be demonstrated in places such as bars 32–4, where a very slight relaxation of the tempo contrasts with a more assertive *a tempo* answer in bars 34–6. Assiduous listening for a consistent tempo across the sections is needed for a sparkling performance.

[A:3] **Mozart** Andante (FL)

Mozart composed this sonata movement aged only 19 but it has all the hallmarks of his mature piano style, including detailed and varied articulation and beautiful cantabile melodies over a murmuring LH.

Counting a quaver pulse (and perhaps marking it on the score) can be an invaluable aid to identifying and correctly playing the rhythm of the RH melody as it flows against mainly LH semiquavers. The LH invites 'finger pedalling' – in which notes are overlapped and connected by the fingers themselves – in order to enrich, but not blur, the harmonies, while the RH sings out with graceful and musically shaped phrases. Listening for the correct balance of hands is a most useful skill in this piece and one that will also help students shape the feminine endings and convey all the expression and articulation marks on the score. How the ornaments are realized may depend on the nimbleness of the student but the overriding principle should be to maintain the tempo of the melodic line while adding elegance.

Imagining the elegant Viennese society in which these sonatas may have been played can contribute to a stylish realization. As well as following the detailed markings, the more musical performances will shape each phrase, consider its direction, and at some points relax the tempo slightly to draw attention to an unexpected harmony or the end of a section. Dynamics were written with the fortepiano in mind, and so will need to be tailored to the heavier modern pianos of today – a passage marked *f* indicates a warmer rather than a harsh sound. With so many notes written it might be tempting to 'hammer' them all out equally, but a more musical effect can be produced with less weight on the shorter notes – semiquavers and demisemiquavers – and more on the longer notes.

A:4 C. P. E. Bach Allegro assai (FL)

🎵 C. P. E. Bach, whose many keyboard works were pivotal in the development of the Classical sonata, was one of the many sons of the great J. S. Bach. He is sometimes known as the 'Berlin Bach' because he spent much of his adult life there employed as the court composer and accompanist to Frederick the Great. This Allegro is an ideal choice for a student who enjoys producing peals of notes.

✋ Achieving a flowing triplet melody – which is largely in the RH – at a consistent tempo can be accomplished by focusing on the RH and establishing a workable fingering. The melody often dances on into the LH and it will be vital to be able to identify where this occurs and then play it, listening carefully to check that there has been a seamless transition in the melody. The crotchet decorations in bars 2–3, 4–5, and similar are not part of the melody, so contrasting the fluid legato of the triplet melody with a light, quieter finger staccato on the crotchets will realize this clearly. Practice involving solid chords in bars 18–22 and subsequent places will help to secure the onward flow and elegant curve of the music, and having both hands poised ready to play with a wrist lift at the end will achieve the seamless arpeggios needed at bars 22, 46, and the final bar. If students have doubts about their ability to maintain the tempo at the trill in bar 45, a mordent may be played instead.

🎨 This dance-like piece will sound most effective at a tempo of $\downarrow$ = 120–26, but bringing in slight rubato in bars 17–18, 41–2, 63–4 and 71–2, and making a controlled ritardando in the final bar, may add definition and style. Getting louder or softer when slowing down is again a matter of personal choice!

A:5 J. S. Bach Giga (FL)

🎵 This stunning Giga, from a partita published during Bach's lifetime in his *Clavierübung,* is a beautiful illustration of a lively jig. On the page it looks to be in two parts but aurally it will be understood as in three, with the LH playing in both an upper and a lower register. The movement involves quick and frequent hand-crossing, so would be a good choice for students with a secure sense of keyboard geography.

✋ Keeping the RH flatter and on the lower part of the keys, and the LH playing further up the keys with curved and poised fingers, will facilitate the hand-crossing. The LH's division into two parts should have the more important top notes singing out and the lower ones quieter, fading from stronger to weaker. Solid work using chords will secure the RH patterns and hand shapes and also encourage dynamic nuances to emerge. Listening to these bars while playing slowly will help make them secure, and writing out the mordents to show where they fit with the RH may also be useful. As always for practice, a slow consistent tempo at first, increasing the speed only when it is secure, will pay dividends.

Looking at some of the excellent examples of gigas being danced on YouTube can help to bring the music alive. There are a range of articulation options for the LH: all notes detached; all slurred in pairs; or lower notes slurred and the higher ones detached, which will emphasize the LH's two parts. Above all, the articulation should be consistent. In terms of dynamics the B section has most of the interest, and, again, while there are several options, students might start *mf* and follow the music's rise and fall, finishing with a crescendo from bar 42 and a stylish allargando as the dance ends. An ideal tempo might be ♩ = 132–44 but at ♩ = 126 a lively effect may still be achieved.

A:6 | **D. Scarlatti** Sonata in D minor — FL

Domenico Scarlatti was born in Naples, Italy, where his father Alessandro was *maestro di cappella* for the royal chapel. Scarlatti served as music teacher to the Portuguese Princess Maria Barbara before moving to the court of Spain in Madrid. He composed over 500 keyboard sonatas for Maria Barbara, all of which are full of rhythmic character and have a wide expressive range. Like most of Scarlatti's sonatas, this one is in binary form and within that form demonstrates a lively but achievable virtuosity.

Scarlatti's trills, in keeping with the conventions of the day, nearly always begin on the upper auxiliary note, even when it means repeating the preceding notes. He is a little inconsistent as to whether or not his trills have a termination such as a turn – some are written in but others not, even when the music appears to need one. The insistent character of the music at bars 8–9 and similar places would imply a trill plus a finishing turn (as in bar 12), whereas this is probably not the case for the other trills. A stylish interpretation of the music will rely on a consistent approach to articulation – for example all the quavers being gently detached – and slow playing and careful listening will establish this. In the places where the LH is close to or above the RH, keeping fingers poised and higher up the keys will prevent a tangle. The large LH leaps of bars 19–26 will benefit from thoughtful fingering and some slow practice, while memorizing the RH will enable students to focus on managing the LH keyboard geography.

There are no editorial dynamics provided on the score and, as always in Baroque music, a variety of interpretations can be considered – terraced dynamics for similar passages, for example, and light and shade as the pitch rises and falls. The movement is marked Allegro, but if played too slowly the music will lack interest; too quickly and it will be untidy. The tempo should therefore be chosen wisely!

B:1 **Delibes** Passepied

The French opera and ballet composer Léo Delibes significantly influenced younger composers including Tchaikovsky, Saint-Saëns and Debussy. His instrumental music remains rather obscure, but deserves wider currency, on the evidence of this exquisite dance movement. It is unquestionably close in terms of characterization, texture and rhythm to the Passepied from Debussy's famous *Suite bergamasque*.

The wide intervallic writing in the LH will benefit from flexibility and relaxation in the wrists. In the outer sections the hands need good independence in order to project contrasted touches. Working initially with all notes in both hands played staccato may help here, making it then easier to realize the RH's two-note slur patterns against the LH staccato. The tempo can be gradually built up, provided that physical comfort and ease remains in place. From bar 26 the held LH thumb notes can be facilitated through using relaxed arm weight, avoiding tightening the wrist. The quavers in both hands in bars 26–33 should be articulated with small, scratching finger movements – keeping hands still and moving fingers out of the keyboard towards the body.

Clarity and transparency are important in conveying the character of this charmingly fleeting piece. The LH *leggiero* figurations may be given subtle colouring through sparing use of the pedal, but caution should be exercised: it may be possible to flutter pedal (lightly raising and lowering the foot in rapid, hovering movements) on the first half of each bar, following this with no pedal for the rest of the bar. Dynamic variation is desirable but should not be overly projected: in the outer sections tonal variation is best kept within the stipulated limits (mostly below *p*). There is a move to *mf* from bar 26 but it could be argued that this louder dynamic applies only to the accented notes and chords within bars 26–33. Certainly it is effective to apply bilateral dynamics here, with staccato quavers continuing with the same tonal approach as used in the opening section.

B:2 **Mendelssohn** Lied ohne Worte (Song without Words)

Felix Mendelssohn's 48 'Songs without Words' may have lost the popularity they once had with the music-loving public, but their charm, immediacy and rich and varied moods remain as impressive as ever. Mendelssohn's virtuoso writing can be highly energized and full of sparkle. This particular number is typical of his filigree virtuosity at its most optimistic and carefree.

For the repeated LH triads in bars 3–4 and elsewhere, experimenting at a *pp* dynamic level with a variety of different triads may prove fruitful, especially if practised without tension, making sure that the fingers feel as though they are moving from the keyboard towards the body as they execute each note. Coordination between the two hands may prove challenging, so it makes sense to work in small segments at first, building up the tempo gradually, before working in larger sections. The two-note slurs in the RH from bar 9 will work well if they are realized as single-movement gestures. The wrist should be relaxed, with the hand lifted in the quaver rest that follows each slur.

The hands should not be balanced too equally here: in order that the characterization remains buoyant and mercurial, the LH needs a consistently light touch. Students should beware of too heavy a LH when its writing becomes more challenging at bars 25–7 and 53–7. Sustaining a steady, reliable pulse throughout is important if the music's structure is to remain clear. Adding accents as stabilizing agents to the first notes of each bar in the LH from bar 9 may facilitate rhythmic control. Though it would be wrong to over-pedal, the music's warmth and colour would be lost with none at all; a compromise solution could involve pedalling only on the first quaver of each beat. It may be useful to employ the *una corda* pedal for the final seven bars.

B:3 **Parry** Elizabeth

Sadly most of Hubert Parry's prolific oeuvre is neglected and unknown today. His unquestionable craftsmanship and idiomatic understanding of the piano is immediately evident in this charming rarity, a musical portrait of the composer's granddaughter which comes from a collection of piano pieces entitled *Shulbrede Tunes*.

Though there are some large stretches, flexibility in the wrists will make most of the figurations comfortable, though those with smaller hands will need to use more pedal to capture the legato markings indicated. However, judicious pedalling will help technical control whatever the size of hand! If the decision is made to change the pedal every two beats the changes need to be made clearly. Students can experiment with pedalling over changes of harmony: taking a group of notes in a continuous pedal is more physically relaxing and takes the strain away from individual notes. Clarity will not be lost if the RH melody line is projected much more strongly than at *mf*, and practising the top part *ff* with everything else *pp* will be beneficial. Bars 10–23 can be performed more easily (and the articulation markings projected more convincingly) if hands are lifted off the keyboard after each beat. Each three-note slur pattern can be thought of as a single movement. In the LH's 10ths and semiquaver flourishes, security can be developed by practising without looking at the hand; indeed, such 'blind practice' will also be useful elsewhere.

The RH phrasing could be seen in parallel to a violinist's bow markings: staccatos can be thought of as (lighter) up-bows and slurs as (stronger) down-bows. Experimentation with rubato may prove fruitful, though this should always be within the context of the initial direction of grazioso. In particular the final three lines, involving a number of tempo changes, should not be over-complicated. It may be useful to play each hand in turn while conducting with the other, making sure that everything flows naturally and rhythmically.

B:4 | **Esplá** Canción de cuna (Lullaby)

📖 Oscar Esplá (1886–1976) was a Spanish composer and student of Saint-Saëns who managed to combine Romantic and nationalistic characteristics in his music with more modern, international influences such as neoclassicism and impressionism. Though several of the pieces in *Suite de pequeñas piezas* look back with respect and love to composers of the past, including Bach and Scarlatti, 'Canción de cuna' seems to be more evocative of the Spanish guitar and folksong.

✋ Practising the top line's melody *f* and legato from bars 16 to 18, keeping the lower RH notes detached and *pp*, will instil a sense of security and control which can then be gradually adjusted into confident playing at the stipulated dynamic level (*ppp*). LH clarity in the legato semiquavers in bars 20–35 can be prepared for by first playing them all staccato. The fingerwork, given more focus and precision through this practice, can then be controlled with greater ease when performed legato as marked. Practising the RH's ornamental notes in bars 20–22 (and similar) by crushing them together with the quaver they precede, then releasing them so that the quaver remains on its own, will be an interesting and effective exercise.

🎨 The main challenge in this delightfully melodic piece relates to tonal control: maintaining *pp* and *ppp* throughout requires confident coordination, including the ability to play with firm fingers but with a slower sense of execution. Taking time to make each note 'speak' should not be a problem if the arms and wrists are relaxed – which is a prerequisite for consistent tone and even playing throughout. Though there are hints and evocations of a full symphony orchestra within the textures, the intimacy and gentle lilting rhythms also evoke the colours of the guitar. A Spanish temperament permeates every phrase. It might therefore be stimulating to imagine the piece performed by a Spanish guitarist who has the powers to evoke a symphonic ensemble!

B:5 | **Gurlitt** Moderato grazioso

📖 The German Romantic composer Cornelius Gurlitt (1820–1901) left a corpus of over 200 opus numbers. He is most famous for his piano miniatures, which were very popular with children, and these charming vignettes are still much played. This beguiling piece is melodically memorable and elegantly written for the instrument.

✋ The arpeggios in the central section may require particular technical preparation if security and control is to be achieved. Working in adjusted rhythms will do wonders in terms of familiarization with the fingering and shifts of hand position: holding the first notes of each bar for much longer durations than written will allow 'brain time' to look ahead and process the position shifts that lie ahead in the bar. Additional technical security with these arpeggios can be cultivated by playing the passage first in block chords. Slow work in these chords must keep the same fingering in place that will be used when returning to play this section as written. In the outer sections, care will be needed with the finger touch to project the importance of the first note of the bar, and to avoid unwanted accents on the resolution of the appoggiatura.

There is a Classical, quasi-minuet poise to the rhythm which gives the piece much of its personality. The upbeat in every phrase unit makes a crescendo towards a mini melodic peak at the start of each bar, then the phrase gradually tapers away with a consistent diminuendo to the end of each phrase mark. Recording practising, to develop sensitive phrasing, will be useful. The first two beats of each bar might instead be taken in a single pedal, and this will work if the LH first beats are realized in semi-staccato guise, quasi pizzicato, as the articulation infers.

B:6 Skryabin Prelude in B flat minor

Skryabin had something of a Chopin obsession: in addition to writing his own sets of Preludes, Études and Mazurkas in evident homage to the Polish master, Skryabin went so far as to quote Chopin's melodic motifs! But his music was never derivative: his early works, of which this Prelude is one, always betray an intensely passionate, late-Romantic Russian aesthetic. Eventually his quest for harmonic exploration and emotional intensity would lead towards a style uniquely his own, one that embraced atonality and elements of mysticism.

Being comfortable with and having control over the wide-ranging, constantly moving LH part is necessary at all stages in the learning process. Even when the music is familiar and securely in place with both hands, continuing work in the LH only may prove invaluable: students should practise overlapping the notes physically so that the articulation is always as smooth and connected as possible. Settling on a good fingering, then sticking to it, is crucial, and it will help to make sure that the thumb always takes the highest note in each group of four LH quavers. Security will develop if larger intervals are given extra space in practice, as if in celebration of them.

Stylistically this music can benefit from subtle rubato, though without losing a strong sense of the pulse. Rhythmic flexibility can be cultivated through singing and breathing – singing each hand separately then imitating the singing on the piano will enable rubato to fall easily into place. It may be inspiring to imagine the LH as a cello, with subtle hairpin dynamic inflections. When the RH is added into the picture, pedalling needs to be sensitively realized. Careful listening will determine how the feet are to be used; students should be prepared to half-pedal and 'flutter' as is necessary, but avoiding *una corda* in every bar!

⌷C:1⌷ **R. R. Bennett** Rosemary's Waltz

Richard Rodney Bennett composed this piece for the 1985 BBC Television dramatization of F. Scott Fitzgerald's final novel, *Tender is the Night*, which deals with the dark issues around obsession, mental illness and descent into alcoholism. Rosemary is one of the main characters, a Hollywood actress on whom the novel's main protagonist is fixated. This waltz cleverly depicts both her sophistication and her apparent elusiveness, with harmonies that are unpredictable, tonal yet lacking an obvious centre. The music beautifully draws on Bennett's skill as an accomplished jazz pianist to conjure the atmosphere of the 1920s, in which the story is set.

With meandering harmonic twists aplenty, care is needed reading the accidentals throughout this wistful piece. The longer arpeggio patterns especially need secure fingering, and it is useful to practise the RH alone, without any pedal, focusing on creating an effective legato line in each phrase. When introducing the pedal, the player will need to ensure that harmonies can linger, but without blurring. Some pedalling indications are given, but the most important thing here is to listen attentively and be led by the ear. Many bars need to be sustained throughout for the full colour of each chord to register, but some others need more frequent pedal changes.

The tempo indication here says it all – the piece should not be hurried, and there is plenty of scope for rubato, a flexibility of pulse contributing to the broader ebb and flow of momentum within phrases. This can be used to underline possible cadence points, for example by holding back slightly in bars 15–16 and 33–4. The *poco rit.* in bar 45 makes this interpretive idea more explicit, underlining the final arrival in F major (the piece starts in G, and doesn't truly settle anywhere after that until the final few bars). The dynamics in the piece must be equally well gauged, and never rise above *mf*, with mini climaxes in bars 26 and 38.

⌷C:2⌷ **Prokofiev** Ridicolosamente (Ridiculously)

Prokofiev's early masterpiece *Visions fugitives* (Fleeting Visions) is a cycle of 20 pithy miniatures that highlight the young composer's ability to turn an effective melodic phrase while exploring fresh piano sonorities. Students may enjoy the thought of playing a piece 'Ridicolosamente' – ridiculously! – but beneath the somewhat acerbic surface this short piece is a brilliant invention, with plenty of melodic interest, vivid colour and spiky wit to hold the musical imagination.

🖐 The key technical challenge of this piece is not the demisemiquavers but rather the awkward hand crossing that is required throughout. At the start, the LH must be positioned towards the back of the black keys, leaving room for the RH, and this becomes increasingly tricky from bar 19, with the LH now on the white keys and moving through a larger arc. It is important to avoid tension within the fingers themselves, and slow practice may be necessary to develop security. Roles between the hands are reversed from bar 31, with the LH playing the melody. As for the demisemiquavers, correctly positioned fingers and a subtle roll of the wrist is all that is needed!

😋 *Ridicolosamente* is a study in rapidly shifting moods, and once the notes are secure, conveying this will become the primary goal of any performance. While Prokofiev's arch humour is perhaps the most striking characteristic, it is important not to lose sight of the lyricism that is always a strong feature in Prokofiev's writing. This can be highlighted in bars 18–22 especially. Prokofiev himself recorded this piece and it may be instructive to listen to the composer's version online, although with a note of caution, as it differs quite noticeably from the printed score. Other interpretations are of course equally valid.

[C:3] **Cheryl Frances-Hoad** Commuterland (AE)

🎹 Anyone who has experienced the bustle of rush hour in a big city will easily relate to the emotions, frustrations and energy that are so brilliantly conveyed in this contemporary study by Cheryl Frances-Hoad. The vivid rhythmic drive certainly captures our attention, right from the start. The composer notes that her piece is in part a homage to Bartók, and there are echoes of the second movement of his Dance Suite here; listening to it will help to place *Commuterland* in a wider musical context.

🖐 The challenge in this piece lies in the constantly changing time signatures, which also quickly alternate between a quaver and a crotchet pulse. The pulse is further obscured by offbeat accents and frequent rests on the first beat. Before students play the notes, it is worth just counting the beats aloud, remembering that quaver beats are twice the speed of the crotchets! This exercise can be repeated along to a recording, and will help instil a sense of the rhythmic dynamism before notes and chords get in the way. Note learning is made easier by memorizing patterns, spotting where and how they recur and are varied. But ultimately, the piece continues to surprise right to the end; highlighting unexpected pattern changes will help students to both communicate and remember the musical narrative.

😋 An effective performance will highlight the drama and virtuosity of Frances-Hoad's extraordinary writing, while convincingly conveying the rhythm. The opening indication *pesante* sets the mood, but also significant are the *leggiero* sections, *subito mp* (for example, from bars 18 and 26). Although the piece starts loudly, there is a considerable range of dynamics from the middle of the piece onwards, and it is important not to lose control, or simply play loud throughout. Emphasizing the many sonic changes will heighten the excitement of the piece, right through to its heart-stopping conclusion!

C:4   **Peter Dickinson**   Hymn-Tune Rag

The exhilarating 'Hymn-Tune Rag' will undoubtedly be a huge hit with all lovers of classic ragtime music! The composer's own recording of the piece was included, along with many others in a similar vein, on his 1986 album *Rags, Blues & Parodies*. He tells us that the style here is modelled on that of the blind American player Charles Hunter (1876–1906), and the syncopations in 'Hymn-Tune Rag' certainly recall those of Hunter's 'Tickled to Death' rag from 1899 (also in the key of A flat major).

The leaping LH of the ragtime style is never an easy trick for pianists to pull off, but the key of A flat helps here, with chord shapes and black keys that are relatively easy for fingers to find. A loose wrist is necessary when managing these jumps, and the weight should be on the bass notes. In the RH, secure fingering will be necessary for managing the runs. Most of the piece is marked *p*, and a light, deft touch will be essential throughout in order to realize this dynamic. When playing the passages in 6ths in the final section, students should keep the RH thumb loose so that it can hop freely from one chord to the next.

Although the time signature is **C**, ragtime is usually in two time, and the metronome mark of ♩ = 100 confirms that the player should aim for a steady two-in-a-bar. Accents on the fourth crotchet, which are such an enjoyable feature of the second section, cut across the beat and can add humour to a performance. The third section is even more syncopated; here the accents can again be exaggerated to add excitement, especially those on the LH octaves. Students should notice that, whereas elsewhere there is a base dynamic of *p*, this section – the piece's climax – is *f* throughout.

C:5   **Khachaturian**   Allegro giocoso

Soviet Armenian composer Aram Khachaturian's music has a very direct impact, and this hugely exciting piece (the first movement of his Sonatina) is no exception. With its quirky use of tonality and impressive-sounding runs it will please pianists and audiences alike. Students may enjoy listening to some of Khachaturian's orchestral ballet scores, which will help them understand the composer's use of colour. As with much of Khachaturian's music, throughout the Sonatina we see the influence of native folk-music idioms and dance. However, the syncopations (e.g. from bar 20) more likely point to the influence of the music and rhythms he encountered during his concert tour of Latin America in 1957.

This is a classic example of a piece that is far easier to play than it sounds – a happy combination that is always popular! However, initial slow practice will allow players to avoid unnecessary problems and untidiness developing later. Memorizing patterns can be a particularly useful strategy – not only in the opening bars, but also in the *poco tranquillo* section from bar 31, where care must be taken not to trip over the descending chromatic figurations. The LH broken-octave pattern at the start is marked *stacc. quasi pizz.*, indicating that the notes should be not only short but light, emulating the pizzicato playing of stringed instruments. The full-octave scales from bar 16 are a contrast to this; including a dash of pedal on the first beat of each bar as written will emphasize this development. A loose wrist is required for success here, and to avoid tension.

An impressive performance of this piece is more than simply a matter of speed – it needs effective dynamic contrasts and good management of the tempo and mood changes. (It can be assumed that the *poco animato* indications in bars 36, 40 and 42 finish at the bar-line each time.) The composer has carefully notated a range of articulations, including legato slurs, staccato, accents, tenuto and marcato, and these must be observed. In the syncopated passages, good accents and the *non legato* will spell out the intended rhythmic effect.

[C:6] **Christopher Norton** Mambo (AE)

Christopher Norton's series of Preludes is a great source of music in a range of styles for players at this level who want to broaden their music horizons, with titles including Jazz, Rock, Country, Eastern, Pacific and Latin Preludes, from which this highly enjoyable 'Mambo' comes. Within the pantheon of Latin American dances, the mambo is a fast, hard-edged, syncopated dance which originated in Cuba in the 1930s and often included improvised moves. While a smoother version known from hit songs such as 'Mambo No. 5' has been popular since the 1950s, this piece takes no prisoners with its intense drama and exciting momentum.

This is a piece for the player with larger hands, as *ff* chords of four notes spanning an octave are a regular feature. The RH will need control to ensure that within chordal passages the top melody line is still emphasized, and the other notes voiced effectively. The octaves in bars 77–8 should use the legato fingerings as written, if possible. Grace notes should be crushed on the beat throughout, and the RH motif in bars 34–5 (and subsequently) benefits from use of alternate fingers 1-3. Precise pedalling in time with the repeated LH chords from bar 63 onwards may need special practice; the intention here is to enlarge the tone rather than sustain the chords beyond their length.

Norton goes to great lengths in his Preludes to include all the articulation, dynamics and pedalling required to convey the varied styles of his pieces, and this 'Mambo' is no exception. It's therefore important to observe every staccato dot and every rest – also to make sure that notes are sufficiently clipped to evoke the mambo rhythm. The *mf* lyrical sections need to be an effective contrast, and pedalling avoided except where written. Students will need to resist the temptation to get carried away with the *ff* excitement of the piece, and keep something in reserve for the big ending!

GRADE 8

J. S. Bach Sarabande and Gigue

Bach's dance movements for keyboard present a unique synthesis of national styles. His music fuses elements from the German, Italian and French traditions, creating a legacy for keyboard players that has proved universal and inspirational on not only a technical but a musical, indeed spiritual, level.

Practising the Sarabande from the beginning without pedal will be helpful. As well as ensuring that fingering is secure, a non-pedal approach encourages care and precision over every sound that is produced. In fact, adopting finger legato throughout is possible, and there is no need to pedal at all. The ornamentation is best worked at in isolation, making sure that fingers that are not playing remain still and relaxed. Synchronization between the hands from bar 5 in the Gigue also requires economy of movement. It would be useful here to practise using contrasting articulation in each hand – staccato in the LH with legato in the RH then reversing the process. Similarly, playing one hand *f* and the other *p* in alternation will promote independence of hands. Early on, the Gigue may benefit from regular metronome practice, possibly starting at ♪ = 104 and gradually speeding up.

In the Sarabande students can enjoy 'placing' the second beats at ends of phrases (e.g. bars 2, 8, 12). The Gigue risks running away in performance, so a strong sense of rhythmic poise is essential. Allowing the music to breathe, and celebrating all the cadences, will imbue the rhythmic flow with clarity and character. Pleasure can be taken in all first beats of this highly energized piece, not hurrying away from each bar's strongest note; care should be taken, however, to avoid accenting each beat of the bar, which will destroy the piece's mercurial grace. The ornamentation suggestions in both movements should not be allowed to restrict creativity: the music affords an opportunity to add further embellishments, provided that they do not distort the pulse or reduce the clarity of the melodic lines.

D. Scarlatti Sonata in D

Domenico Scarlatti's extraordinary legacy of over 500 keyboard sonatas contains some of the most challenging and individual music in the repertoire. Perhaps it was Scarlatti's isolation in Spain that spurred his originality and innovation as a composer, leading him towards figurations, harmonic progressions and technical challenges that still surprise listeners today.

This music is typical of Scarlatti in that clarity, transparency and rhythmic security are prerequisites. Finger independence is an important technical asset to develop. Building confidence in moving position in arpeggios will also be beneficial. The ornaments should be isolated and worked at with fingers close to the keys, moving only the fingers that are playing notes and keeping the hand as still on the keyboard as possible. Practising 'blind' could be useful for building facility. Working in half-bar units with an emphasis on clear articulation and physical comfort will also help, especially if beginning slowly and gradually getting faster. Synchronization between the hands may prove challenging in bar 6 and elsewhere: it will be much easier to articulate the ornaments clearly and evenly if fingers are on the keys just a little in advance of playing the notes.

This sonata may be imagined orchestrally, and students might try to recreate the effect of, for example, trumpets and lower brass (bar 1), flutes and other upper woodwind (bar 2 onwards), even guitars (bars 10–12), and drums (closing bars in each half). Small musical units immediately repeated call for echo effects (bars 2–3, 4–5), and the crunchy minor 2nds from bar 13 can be enjoyed and projected fully. The double notes and octaves (e.g. bars 31–6 and 53–8) should remain within the light, crystalline context of the sonata as a whole. Indeed, heaviness should be avoided at all costs, keeping weight away from the LH, which can take arpeggiated chords at times if desired. Players might vary which chords are arpeggiated and which aren't, and experiment with the chords in bars 10–12 and 41–5.

A:3 **Shostakovich** Prelude and Fugue in A minor (MM)

Written in 1950–1, Shostakovich's 24 Preludes and Fugues, Op. 87, last for over 150 minutes in performance and stand alongside Hindemith's *Ludus tonalis* and Busoni's *Fantasia contrappuntistica* at the summit of contrapuntal music for keyboard.

Metronome practice might be useful for the Prelude, especially if it is set initially at a very slow speed (possibly ♩ = 52) and then gradually extended. This will help avoid hesitations! Beginning the Fugue slowly is advisable too, and after work isolating each voice and each hand, practising with a staccato touch for every note, then a totally legato touch, will develop finger strength as well as familiarity with the notes. Mastering the Fugue's many leaps will involve selecting some intervals for specific practice, and practising without looking at the keyboard.

The Prelude's opening semiquaver rest can be confusing and distort the pulse, but an accent on the second beat of the opening bar will make the rhythmic logic clear. It might also help to hear the first beat of each bar mentally. Pedal is not needed, and students should strive for a fantastic *leggiero* touch throughout. Although a countermelody is not marked until bar 25 (tenuto crotchets), a melody line can be projected from within the semiquavers – initially this could be practised with the fifth finger alone. Carefully communicating all the Fugue's articulation markings can give tremendous characterization.

In both Prelude and Fugue clarity and rhythmic control are priorities, so slightly slower tempos enabling control are infinitely preferable to speeds that cannot be sustained comfortably. In the Fugue pedalling should tonally enhance the music rather than distort its inherent transparency and its texture: the middle pedal can be used for the low F♯ in bar 38, and the marked accents will be enhanced if taken in the sustaining pedal with short, fast movements.

Though many interpretive approaches are possible for both Prelude and Fugue it may help to conceive of them in terms of physical movement. Students might record performances and then dance while listening back.

[A:4] J. S. Bach Prelude and Fugue in A minor (FL)

Bach's *The Well-Tempered Clavier* constitutes some of the most significant keyboard music written, and it forms a core part of many pianists' repertoire. This Prelude and Fugue would be a good choice for students who have enjoyed playing Bach's Two-Part Inventions and would like a further challenge! The two could not present a greater contrast: the introspective Prelude with its chromaticisms and contrapuntal features is followed by one of Bach's grandest and most rhythmically energetic fugues.

The editorial suggestion of *dolce ma espressivo* for the Prelude is an appropriate one, and a legato cantabile touch throughout will achieve this. Playing hands separately and listening assiduously should help to produce the flowing independence of hands that is required. Gently pointing out the two main themes in bar 1 – the rising octave followed by the descending chromatic quavers in the LH, and the descending chromatic figure of demisemiquavers and semiquavers in the RH – will demonstrate stylistic awareness. The bass trill at the end of the A section, in bar 16, will benefit from slow and counted practice together with the RH, while a small rallentando here may help students navigate the notes, and also sound expressive.

The Fugue's subject (first appearance in bars 1–3) requires a firmer finger touch supported by a little arm weight, with a lighter countersubject (the demisemiquavers from bar 3) always flowing towards the longer notes. Four-note demisemiquaver trills should be quite possible at a steady eight quavers per bar, provided that a suitable fingering is decided on and adhered to, although other approaches are of course possible. The mountainous bass-line ascent (commencing in bar 18), with the effective suggested fingering meticulously observed, provides the climax of the piece, and is accompanied by a RH two-part dialogue.

Listening to recordings and also considering orchestral colours will help students make decisions about articulation and dynamics; a consistent execution of these will identify the more secure and stylish performances. Achieving a complete contrast of moods between Prelude and Fugue is vital, and taking time between the movements in performance will reinforce this.

A:5 | **Handel** Fugue No. 6 in C minor (FL)

Handel was equally famous as a composer and as one of the most eminent keyboard players of the day. His name is not the first to spring to mind in connection with Baroque fugues, but this collection of Six Fugues, written early in his career, ranks among his finest keyboard works. This Fugue is a delight to play, as Handel masterfully takes us through the four-voice *stretto* fugue (a fugue in which the subject entries overlap and 'pile up'), ending with a majestic conclusion.

The first step is to find and mark the fugue's subject – its first entry occupies bars 1–3 – wherever it occurs. A useful next step would be to decide on the subject's articulation and shape and isolate each occurrence in practice to ensure that it is played consistently. Time spent in separate-hands practice and also on the individual voices will enable the threads to be disentangled. Areas of focus may be suggested by the movement's three sections (the second begins after the cadence in bars 25–6; the third after the interrupted cadence in bars 43–4), and giving particular attention to the *stretti* in bars 14–16, 27–32, 33–6, 44–9 and 57–60, where the subject and parts of the subject tumble over themselves, will help to secure fluency and confidence.

An effective articulation would be a cantabile playing of the subject as it rises towards the RH's fifth-finger G and then gently detaching the four quavers of that bar as the subject makes way for the second entry in the bass. Deciding on and writing in the fingering at an early stage will be helpful. No dynamics are on the score but stylish performances will clearly but gently point out the subject but also have a rise and fall in shaping throughout the Fugue. The Adagio at the very end indicates a clear broadening out of the speed, giving the piece a real sense of conclusion – which might also involve a crescendo or diminuendo. Whatever choice is made needs to be convincingly delivered!

A:6 | **Hindemith** Praeludium (FL)

Hindemith's mighty *Ludus tonalis* (Tone Games), composed in 1942 in America, is a set of 12 fugues that are connected by interludes, framed by a prelude and postlude. The Prelude in C has a broad and spacious introduction followed by four differing sections, and travels from C to F sharp. Improvisatory in character and less daunting than it initially may appear on the page, this would be an excellent option for the student who enjoys using the entire keyboard and is at ease with the dissonant tensions and spacious lyricism of this style.

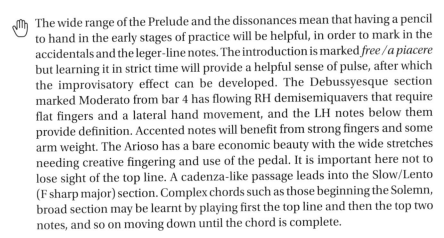

The wide range of the Prelude and the dissonances mean that having a pencil to hand in the early stages of practice will be helpful, in order to mark in the accidentals and the leger-line notes. The introduction is marked *free/a piacere* but learning it in strict time will provide a helpful sense of pulse, after which the improvisatory effect can be developed. The Debussyesque section marked Moderato from bar 4 has flowing RH demisemiquavers that require flat fingers and a lateral hand movement, and the LH notes below them provide definition. Accented notes will benefit from strong fingers and some arm weight. The Arioso has a bare economic beauty with the wide stretches needing creative fingering and use of the pedal. It is important here not to lose sight of the top line. A cadenza-like passage leads into the Slow/Lento (F sharp major) section. Complex chords such as those beginning the Solemn, broad section may be learnt by playing first the top line and then the top two notes, and so on moving down until the chord is complete.

Listening to other pieces from *Ludus tonalis* will accustom students to the sound-world of Hindemith, while learning a little about his life and the political world of the 1940s may be of benefit in understanding and expressing the music.

[A:7] Mendelssohn Fugue in B flat (FL)

Mendelssohn was one of the finest pianists of his day, an excellent organist and an inspiring conductor, as well as being the composer of works that combined his study of earlier musical styles with the Romantic characteristics of the era. His admiration of Bach influenced the composition of the Six Preludes and Fugues and No. 6 is an example of the Baroque form as a vehicle for bravura passages and much drama. It will suit students who have nimble fingers and who delight in virtuosity.

The reason we play scales is amply demonstrated in this Fugue. Achieving speed and fluency in the semiquaver passages of the subject is likely to be one of the challenges of this piece. It is therefore advisable to mark these entries on the score and practise each voice slowly, with a marked-in fingering, aiming for accuracy and control. The dotted rhythms may be more accurately performed if the semiquaver is thought of as belonging to the dotted quaver. Special care is needed at the points where the subject travels between hands, such as in bar 12, or where the LH takes over in the treble clef (e.g. bar 17). Effective chord playing in bar 20 will benefit from a correct hand-shape before each chord, using strong fingers, and with a flexible wrist and forearm to create the extra volume needed. To create a good sound here and prevent muscular tension, there should be no strain or stiffness.

It would be tempting to play this entirely *f*, but that would result in no feel for the direction of the music. Engaging performances will not only observe the dynamics given but include additional light and shade. The fugue subject might make a crescendo towards the crotchet and then be slightly less forceful as the dotted figuration makes way for more semiquaver runs. A virtuosic, fully accurate performance at ♩ = 132 would be wonderful but a shaped and controlled one at ♩ = 112 would also be extremely effective.

A:8 **Soler** Sonata in D minor (FL)

A disciple of Domenico Scarlatti, the Catalan composer Padre Antonio Soler wrote more than 300 keyboard sonatas, characterized by rhythmic vitality, wide leaps and, for the time, extreme ranges. This sparkling binary-form piece is one of Soler's many sonatas in one movement, and is also a less contrapuntal option than other List A pieces at this grade.

The LH section at bars 31–9 and 105–13 would benefit from chord analysis and some solid chord practice in order to hear more clearly the harmonic progressions and establish the hand patterns needed. It is a good workout for the fourth and fifth fingers but lateral hand movement from fifth finger up to thumb will give these fingers the necessary support and result in a more even tone. The consecutive octaves of bars 40–43 and subsequent places will benefit from a relaxed and balanced forearm, wrist and hand; at any sign of undue tension, stop, shake the arm, and then try again. Practising with eyes shut is a fun and effective way to build confidence. A suitable articulation would consist of detached quavers and articulated, flowing non-legato semiquavers. Doing something different at bars 106–12 will create interest, such as slurring the first two RH quavers and detaching the following ones. How to execute the trills is the next question: a rapid trill starting on the main note was the convention of eighteenth-century Spanish composers, although a crisp inverted mordent would also work well. The overriding aim is not to allow the ornaments to slow down the tempo of this lively piece.

There are many opportunities at repeated phrases and motifs for terraced dynamics, whereas sequential passages (e.g. at bars 8–12) might suggest a subtle diminuendo or crescendo. A sense of lively energy and rhythmic confidence should pervade this piece and will contribute to a stylish performance of what was written as an exciting showpiece for the harpsichord or fortepiano.

B:1 **C. P. E. Bach** Un poco allegro (AE)

C. P. E. Bach, second surviving son of J. S. Bach, was regarded by Haydn, Mozart and Beethoven alike as their great predecessor and architect of classicism. Today his vast treasury of keyboard works remains sadly neglected, and this gem – with its freedom of expression and unexpected structural twists – will be a magical discovery for many. It is the opening movement from the second of Bach's six Württemberg Sonatas, dating from 1744 – an important collection that followed his set of Prussian Sonatas (1742) and cemented his growing reputation at the court of Frederick II of Prussia. Listening to the whole sonata is recommended – the second movement is sublime!

The keyboard writing here is a fascinating amalgam of Baroque passagework and ornamentation with Classical phrasing and expression, perfectly encompassing the fluid transition from the old style to the new. Originally written for the clavichord, the passages in 3rds and 6ths are not easy to realize evenly on the modern piano, the demisemiquavers in bar 4 giving an early indication of the challenge ahead. Players should lean into the dotted quaver here, lifting and releasing any weight for the demisemiquavers themselves. Lightness of touch must dominate throughout, and care should be taken to avoid a forced tone and any build-up of tension in the semiquaver passages.

The modest tempo indication – 'a little fast' – should be noted: the sense of shape, phrasing and expression will soon be lost if the piece is played too quickly. Articulation will benefit from being non-legato, but not strictly detached. Upper mordents can be interpreted as upper-note acciaccaturas throughout, while the appoggiaturas should be expressive 'sighs', leaning on the grace note rather than the main note. The longer trill included in the first adagio pause (bar 13) can be lengthened, and similar trills may be added at will by the performer in subsequent adagio bars later in the piece.

B:2 **Beethoven** Presto alla tedesca (AE)

Though a mature work, Beethoven's Sonata in G major, Op. 79, has a largely untroubled Classical charm that is reminiscent of his earlier works. One of his easier sonatas, perhaps because Clementi had asked him to compose it to be so, it was described by Beethoven himself as a 'sonate facile' or 'sonatina'. The title 'Presto alla tedesca' anticipates the 'Alla danza tedesca' fourth movement of the String Quartet Op. 130, the opening motif of which is an exact inversion of this opening. The character of a *deutscher Tanz*, a fast dance in waltz time, pervades the movement, while Beethoven's wit shines right through to the throwaway ending.

It is tempting to see that rare tempo indication – Presto – and launch into this movement at breakneck speed, but there is a point at which any performance will sound rushed and lacking clarity (for a truly audacious tempo players might listen to Pollini, who opts for around $\downarrow$. = 100 in his 1989 recording). Some caution is therefore advised; it will be necessary to hear inwardly the most difficult passage before setting the opening pulse. That passage will, for most, be the Development section, bars 52–122. Here the LH jumps and crossing hands pose a challenge. It is worth considering why Beethoven wrote the passage this way, rather than giving the treble-clef notes to the RH.

It should be noted, too, that this passage is marked *dolce*, and is the primary place in the movement where Beethoven asks for pedalling.

Beethoven's music is essentially dramatic, and delivery of the contrasts in the dynamics – themselves limited to *f*, *p*, *cresc.* and *dim.* – is therefore of the utmost importance. Students should notice, too, his use of *leggiermente*, *dolce* and the frequent *sf* signs, all of which contribute to the narrative. The composer was less precise with his notation of articulation, so we can assume that any staccato and legato suggestions he offers are to be applied consistently. Care will be needed to play the ending softly; it is noticeable that no rallentando has been indicated.

B:3 **Schubert** Allegro moderato   (AE)

One of Schubert's sunniest piano sonatas, the unfinished E major D. 459 was written in August 1816, when he was just 19 years old. Youthful optimism may pervade this charming movement, but so too does a determination to demonstrate his compositional prowess. The movement is characterized by a typically beautiful song-like melody, with contrapuntal inner lines that foreshadow his later sonatas, and shows a mastery of the extended sonata form developed by Beethoven. Also known as *Fünf Klavierstücke* (Five Piano Pieces), the work was published posthumously in 1846. Whether or not the five movements were conceived to belong together remains unknown. However, in Schubert's surviving autograph this first piece, Allegro moderato, was titled Sonata, so whatever the purpose of the remaining movements his original intention here is clear.

This piece, like so many of Schubert's sonata movements, is rather more difficult than first impressions suggest. Large hands will be a benefit here, not only helping with the general stretches and larger chords that appear, but also facilitating the control of sometimes dense inner voicing and counterpoint. Avoiding tension is essential, especially as the piece requires a dynamic palette of predominately softer hues. It is important to observe the rests, which, as well as punctuating the music, offer a chance for the wrists to breathe.

Beautiful phrasing will bring rewards, as will control of the texture, and playing with restraint. A relaxed tempo can allow Schubert's gorgeous melodies to linger in the imagination, but without either becoming too indulgent or losing sight of the work's Classical roots. Half-pedalling, avoiding any blurring, will give the tone a warm haze, but it is useful to practise without pedal to help develop management of the fingering patterns and legato line. In the fairly short Development section a very different, darker and more mysterious mood can be conveyed, and with genuine drama in the *ff* of bar 62. This will help give the performance shape.

B:4 **Clementi** Presto

Clementi's magisterial Sonata in F minor, Op. 13 No. 6, from 1785 shows his originality, superb understanding of the instrument, and ability to develop memorable material. This sonata's finale must have had a significant impact on Beethoven, because its opening melody was later used as the theme of the 'Eroica' Symphony's finale. In fact, the whole of this quietly energized movement seems Beethovenian in terms of its concentrated, obsessively searching characterization.

Velocity can be built up in this bravura movement by working up to the ideal speed in micro units. The outsized cross-hand LH leaps (such as in bars 24–5, 30–31 and 102–3) should be practised in isolation until they feel comfortable; slow, quiet repetition will instil an awareness of keyboard geography that leads naturally to reliability and confidence in this. The 3rds and Alberti figurations in bars 74–99 require rotary movement, and the many LH octave passages will need relaxed arm weight if they are to be realized with comfort and ease.

Performances will benefit from celebrating the extreme dynamic contrasts and projecting each one that Clementi requests on the score. Prior to Clementi, keyboard scores tended to be very spartan in terms of instructions for dynamics and articulation, and much of the drama here comes solely from these epoch-making instructions. Overuse of the sustaining pedal throughout should be avoided, as the textures risk becoming too resonant and heavy. However, the octave passages need to be bound together through deft footwork, with pedal perhaps best utilized between notes. Such 'binding' dabs of pedal will make for a neater aesthetic than longer pedalling through groups of notes. An overlapping touch – 'finger pedalling' – will also enable resonance while retaining clarity and control of the semiquaver scalic runs and rotary figurations. The piece's character requires movement and energy, and to achieve this, students must find an opening tempo that is not too ambitious.

B:5 **Haydn** Moderato

'Sturm und Drang' (Storm and Stress) was a movement in literary and musical circles from the 1760s until the 1780s. Music that it influenced tended to be in the minor rather than the major, with an emphasis on extreme contrasts of mood and emotion as well as a tendency towards angularity and instability. Haydn's Sonata in C minor, Hob. XVI/48, of 1789 can be considered as part of this movement; it contains drama, pathos and innovation aplenty.

It will be important to come to terms as early as possible with the rotary movements (largely in the LH) and the four-against-three rhythms in bars 32–4, 47–64 and 93–6. One strategy would be to lean on the lowest bass notes in these passages, extending them into quavers and 'finger-pedalling' with them so that they overlap each other; this will provide a stable anchor for technical control. Practice of the RH's four-note demisemiquaver flourishes with the LH triplets, patiently and in isolation, will yield results. Working via many repetitions will be beneficial if done initially with a quiet dynamic and a slow tempo. Playing with physical ease is essential for long-term success. In bars 26–7 the two-note slurs in a 'Scotch snap' rhythm may be easily dispatched if weight is added to the first note then released on the second.

Musically this sonata requires a large expressive range. Students need to be aware of losing tempo when the ornamentation becomes more involved (from bar 9) – and ornamentation overall will work well if it is realized on the beat rather than before it (the first examples are in bars 2, 3 and 4). The cadenza sections beginning in bars 24 and 87 can be as free and as daring as possible. There is no need for the deployment of the sustaining pedal anywhere in this music, as sostenuto may also be found via overlapping legato and strength in the fingers.

B:6   **Haydn**   Rondo: Presto

Haydn's Sonata in C major, Hob. XVI/36, from 1771 comprises two movements that are strikingly contrasted. While the Moderato opening movement is declamatory, deeply expressive and full of dramatic contrasts, this Rondo: Presto finale is a comedy of manners.

Many of the technical challenges will be overcome if articulation and execution are limited to fingerwork allied with loose wrists. Care should be taken to avoid using significant arm weight and to keep as close as possible to the keys. The 6ths in bars 10–11 will flow more easily if the lower notes are played staccato while the upper notes are bound together with finger legato. The semiquaver passagework in bars 73–9 can be practised and made more secure if the fifth finger is made pivotal, holding onto each note for as long as possible. Rotary movement will help to make the LH broken-octave writing in bars 83–6 more manageable.

It is important to project all the details throughout the movement, particularly in each presentation of the rondo theme, showing the staccatos, two-note slurs and longer phrase markings clearly – they do so much to instil character and personality into the music. Where no articulation marks are present (as in the semiquaver passagework in bars 63–7) slurs and staccatos may be added. These can emulate a violinist's bowing, with slurs corresponding to down-bows and staccatos to (lighter) up-bows. Tonally a *leggiero* approach is desirable everywhere. Even the LH octaves, broken octaves and filled octaves in bars 70–87, 194–7 and 238–55 should be approached in terms of drawing the hand towards the body when executed. Within the broad dynamic markings it is possible to add shading, further contrasts and inflections. Careful deployment of the sustaining pedal at climaxes and cadences may be helpful, and some overlapping of notes in the LH during the C minor episode will achieve resonance without sacrificing clarity in the RH.

B:7 Kuhlau Allegro

This substantial sonata allegro shows the craftsmanship, pianistic elegance and immediacy of this composer at his best. Friedrich Kuhlau is a significant figure in the development of the keyboard sonata, and his sonatas have proved excellent vehicles for the technical development of pianists. The melodic material presented in this sonata is full of contrasts and will make a convincing impression in performance if the pianist has the ability to control the pulse and an understanding of how to project different dynamics and touches.

Perhaps the most striking technical feature of the piece is the need for rotary movement. This technique, which requires a concentrated, economical approach as well as relaxed wrists, can be adopted for semiquaver passagework in both hands. It is advisable to take a slow tempo in the early stages before gradually increasing speed. Elsewhere there is a call for sparkling brilliance via strong fingerwork in the *f* scale passages in places such as bars 24–5 and 31–2, along with a developed control and confidence in some of the semiquaver flourishes that are presented at a quieter dynamic level. The latter may be negotiated easily if the articulation adopted includes a mixture of two-note slurs with staccato, rather than everything being played in a single legato gesture (see bars 39 and 47).

This movement thrives on rhythmic control and extreme contrasts, presented with an energetic positivity! Making the most of the differences between the main melodic content and the subsidiary voices will provide colour. When the texture becomes involved, it is possible to experiment with contrasting colours. Different touches can be tried in each part: in bars 5–10, for instance, realizing the top voice at *f*, the lowest semibreve bass notes at *mf*, and then the middle bass-clef notes at *p* or even *pp* will make the music both clearer and more characterful.

B:8 Mozart Rondo: Allegretto

Towards the end of his life Mozart's style began to embrace much more contrapuntal experimentation, and though the climax of this tendency is unquestionably the finale of his last symphony (the 'Jupiter'), this sonata, dating from 1788, shows a subtle deployment of imitative devices and textures. Polyphony is especially important in the concluding 25 bars of this Rondo.

Perhaps the most challenging passage of the movement occurs towards the end, in bars 152–69. This can be practised in half-bar segments, with the aim of strongly projecting each minim. Finger substitution may be used on these longer legato notes along with a lighter non-legato touch for the quavers. Elsewhere clarity and control in the RH triplet semiquavers (bars 59, 61, etc.) and demisemiquavers (bars 66 and 67) can be developed by practising in small musical units. The best effect will be achieved by keeping the hand still and only moving the fingers that are playing notes – the others should be kept stationary and relaxed!

It is essential to project a consistent, unified pulse throughout, but the movement can work convincingly at several different tempos. Starting too fast is inadvisable – for any slowing down later (e.g. in bars 27–38) will severely affect the structural integrity of the interpretation. Finding a speed at which the most technically awkward passages can be dispatched with ease, and beginning the movement at that tempo, is essential to both effective practice and a convincing performance.

In terms of texture and contrasts the use of the pedal can be helpful, though there is much that can and should be explored via the fingers rather than the feet – pedalling is not actually necessary anywhere in the movement, as contrasts can also be projected via articulation. In the contrapuntal F minor section (bars 95–116) the marked legato lines can be nicely offset with non-legato articulation elsewhere. This will make the passage sound more multi-textured, and highlight the imitation.

C:1 Chopin Nocturne in G minor

Chopin's Nocturnes remain hugely popular, and Op. 37 No. 1 in G minor is one of the most beautifully melodic. The pensive G minor theme that opens the piece leads to a more persuasive B flat major from bar 9. This material is repeated with variation, the opening G minor melody returning a third time with Chopin's characteristic filigree decoration. There is then a central hymn-like melody in E flat, before the return of the main material. The piece is a perfect example of structural economy and melodic beauty, and is sure to win the hearts of players and audiences alike.

To ensure that the RH melody is cantabile throughout, students should consider playing with flatter fingers than usual, consciously transferring arm weight from one note to the next, all the while maintaining supple wrists and free elbows. The more decorative runs require a lighter touch, and it helps to memorize the patterns here – for example, in bars 36 and 86 noticing that the chromatic passage gives way to a descending diminished 7th, finishing with a rising F major scale. The chords in the middle section should also be legato, emphasizing the upper line, and practice without the pedal will be both revealing and helpful.

Although marked Lento, the piece should not begin too slowly, or the subsequent repetitions and variations on the melody will appear indulgent. Here it may help to think of the minim, rather than the crotchet, as determining the inner heartbeat. It is essential to pay close attention to Chopin's phrasing marks, as these underpin the flow of the music, and can be used as a guide for rubato. Time 'robbed' from one part of the phrase should be made up elsewhere, ensuring consistent flow. Rubato is often needed for the grace notes, which should (according to Chopin) be played directly on the beat, with the bass note.

C:2 **Debussy** Voiles (Sails)   (AE)

The title *Voiles* is usually translated as 'Sails', and it is easy to picture a boat becalmed at sea, with – towards the middle of the piece – a gentle breeze rising to fill the sails. However, the title could equally be translated as 'Veils', the piece perhaps evoking the effects created by American dancer Loie Fuller (1862–1928), whose experimentation with diaphanous silk costumes and colourful lighting effects was a sensation in Paris around the time the piece was composed. A silent movie sequence of Fuller's dancing can be viewed online, and may inspire the imagination of those approaching this piece.

This piece is a favourite with analysts, as Debussy uses the whole-tone scale almost exclusively, switching to the pentatonic for the short central section. This achievement poses unique problems for the player, the writing demanding different fingering patterns from the standard archetypes familiar from major and minor keys. This challenge is compounded by the frequent use of 3rds, and it may help to experiment with alternative fingerings, looking at a variety of editions.

Pedalling is also a particular challenge. There must be sufficient sustaining to ensure that the tolling B♭ ostinato is ever-present, but without losing clarity elsewhere in the texture. The first edition (Durand, 1910) includes no pedalling marks except for the indication to hold the pedal throughout the final three bars, clearly an intended special effect.

One might think that there would be considerable freedom of interpretation in this piece, heralded by the opening instruction to play 'in a rhythm without strictness'. In fact, Debussy provides plenty of expressive detail and performing instruction, which should be followed closely. The piece has a broadly ternary structure, the narrative beginning enshrouded in stillness. The middle section lasts from bar 42 to bar 47, and here the tempo is faster, the writing switches from whole-tone to pentatonic scales, and the dynamic rises to *f*. Emphasizing these contrasts will make any performance far more persuasive.

C:3 **Nikolay Kapustin** Sonatina, Op. 100 (AE)

With one foot in the classical tradition and the other in the world of jazz, it is no wonder that Nikolay Kapustin's virtuosic piano music draws from both. However, the composer insists he is not a jazz pianist, and claims no interest in improvisation, preferring to perfect his own music on paper. This Sonatina is the result of a commission from a children's music school, who requested something 'not too difficult'. Initially Kapustin declined, but he subsequently relented, delivering this charming and accessible work which skilfully combines many of the standard tropes of the Viennese Classical sonatina with his own trademark jazz rhythms and humour.

Aside from the challenge that the notes alone present – and these must be addressed with meticulous, slow practice – a priority here will be to pay close attention to the slurs, phrasing, and other articulations. That the piece often requires different articulation in each hand simultaneously can prove especially difficult, and needs particular care. The many written accents add considerably to the sense of style, and it is worth experimenting to see how much these can be exaggerated. They are often the engine of the syncopation that dominates the Latin-infused rhythm.

This piece presents such a smorgasbord of vivid musical ideas that the performer must consider carefully how to integrate them into the whole. A consideration of the Classical structure provides a suitable starting point, and, in particular, emphasizing the lyrical qualities at the start of the second subject (bar 19), its playful continuation, and the forced syncopation of the codetta will help spell out the structure to the listener. Similarly, the *rit.* and Andante that precede the Recapitulation, with their Haydnesque humour, can be exploited to the full. The tempo should not be rushed, but players need to be aware of the minim beat of the ¢ time signature.

C:4 **Martinů** Prélude en forme de Danse (FL)
(Prelude in the form of a dance)

This wonderfully energetic Prelude with its dissonances and offbeat driving rhythms is likely to suit students who have relished playing pieces from Bartók's *Mikrokosmos* or are familiar with Shostakovich's *Dances of the Dolls*. Written in 1929, it reflects the changing musical times by juxtaposing folksong-like melodies, repetition, unexpected rhythms and frequent percussive piano effects.

The absence of time signature can be daunting – and yet also freeing! In the early stages of learning, counting quavers and drumming out the rhythmic pattern of short sections on the piano lid will be enormous fun; this will not only secure the rhythms but will embed the dynamics and articulation before attempting to play them on the keys. The complex chord passages, for example in bars 14–17, can be learnt by breaking them down into short sections, securing the fifth finger, then the thumb notes, before adding the inner notes and finally the LH. A slightly higher wrist will give the extra weight and dynamic needed in the *f* and *ff* passages. The shapes for the chords can be prepared by slow practice, sometimes in pairs, and this will also lead to greater fluency. The suggested tempo is quick but achievable with metronome practice starting at ♩ = 130 and progressing in stages to ♩ = 168. However, an effective Allegro vivo with details of articulation and dynamics could also be communicated at ♩ = c. 152.

It would be tempting to play this piece *f* and marcato throughout, but each section has its own character and the more sophisticated performances will demonstrate this. For example, the folksong-like melody of bar 18 is lighter and more melodic, the *p* at bar 33 benefits from a lighter staccato touch, and the third page has many moments of lyricism and tonal light and shade. Listening to the other preludes in the set, and also to Stravinsky's *Rite of Spring* and *Petrushka*, will open up this exciting sound-world.

C:5 | **Rachmaninoff** Elégie (Elegy) FL

Rachmaninoff's Romantic style combined with Russian nationalism and often flavoured with melancholy is beautifully distilled into this Elégie. Often overshadowed by the Prelude in C sharp minor from the same set, it is a more reflective, rhapsodic work with rich sonorities and a wide expressive range. This is a fabulous option for students who can manage the chords, and enjoy sensuous melodies and rich harmonies.

In the piece's outer sections the LH has to travel up to three-and-a-half octaves. This will be aided by a workable fingering, legato pedalling and the forearm's ability to travel from left to right and back again usually using fingers 2 or 3 as pivots. A feeling for the geography of the keyboard will help lateral freedom. Differentiating the many layers and showing what is background and what is foreground will characterize the most musical performances; for example, arm weight will help the opening RH melody sound over the many deeper LH notes and encourage a singing LH melody in the Più vivo section. The *appassionato* climax at bars 70–82 has three layers: most important is the RH melody, then the bell-like LH low octave A, and then the LH quaver chords which provide supportive onward movement. The RH's complex chords here can be made fluent by practising first the fifth-finger notes, before adding the thumb and finally the inner fingers – always watching out for tension and, should it appear, stopping to 'shake out' the arm.

The full gamut of dynamics and emotions is displayed in this passionate lament, from *ppp* to *fff*. A suitably expressive Romantic performance may be inspired by developing a narrative, imagining either the Russian landscape and seasons or the emotions evoked by the life that was lost. Performances of the Elégie will illustrate the Romantic sensibility required, and Rachmaninoff himself playing this can be found on YouTube alongside recordings of the cello arrangement, which amply demonstrate where the expressive and sonorous melodies lie.

C:6 Raymond Yiu Lullaby (for Edna Trident Hornbryce) (FL)

Raymond Yiu, who began piano lessons aged four and started composing as a teenager, studied electrical and electronic engineering before eventually becoming a full-time musician. He has composed orchestral and instrumental works and had a symphony commissioned for the Proms and performed in the 2015 season. This beautiful melancholy Lullaby to the memory of Richard Rodney Bennett would suit students who have a facility for lyricism and enjoy playing music in an approachable contemporary style.

A cantabile sound in LH and RH can be achieved by transferring weight from finger to finger, with some arm weight added in louder passages, and by constant listening to the tone produced and the balance between the hands. Differentiating between the cantabile melodies, the bell-like dotted minims of the bass clef and the subtly shifting inner harmonies will mark out the more nuanced performances. There is a gentle waltz feel to the piece hinted at by the tenuto LH (dotted minims and minims) and some of the RH articulation marks. With the return of the main melody at bar 63 (a magical point), a 6th lower than the original, the LH is positioned higher than the RH. To avoid a tangle of fingers the LH fingers should be kept curved and placed towards the top of the keys, with the RH fingers flatter and lower down the keys.

The dynamic markings are helpfully detailed, and a musical realization of them will result in an improvisatory-sounding and relaxed ebb and flow of ideas and harmonies. Making sure that the *mf* and *f* are brief and never harsh will contribute to the Lullaby's overall sad mood, and observing the *molto rit.* in the final two bars – possibly adding a tiny pause to the final note – will allow this elegy to drift away.

C:7 L. Boulanger Cortège (MM)

The early death of Lili Boulanger (1893–1918) deprived the world of a major compositional talent. The French composer's legacy amounts to only 50 works, including some highly evocative piano miniatures. Boulanger was often able to use familiar figurations and chords in new ways, finding a pathway to originality in the process. 'Cortège', the final number in a collection of *Trois morceaux*, is a mercurial flight of fancy, a fantastic étude in *leggiero* pianism that explores strikingly beautiful harmonies and pianistic figurations while retaining a robust and incisively rhythmic march motif.

Small hands may find it challenging to cope with the LH figurations. They can be made easier by pivoting from the pad of the finger on each beat's central semiquaver note – swivelling round so that the elbow moves the whole forearm into position. Any sensation of stretching is best avoided. Judicious use of the sustaining pedal in small but frequent dabs will prove extremely useful, enabling seamless changes of position that might otherwise sound ungainly. Bars 33–4 require a greater sonority which can be achieved if the hands are lifted quickly off the keys while keeping the pedal down – an effect almost of the music being lifted out from the keyboard. This should enable players to project the long-held C♯ in the middle voice above the swirling semiquavers.

This dream-like evocation requires small amounts of pedal to create the requisite sense of fantasy and wonder. Being overly articulate with the semiquavers in each hand should be avoided: they can be presented as washes of colour, enabling the music to take flight in a most exotic way. The rhythmic characterization inherent in the melodic line is distinctive, but a sense of mystery may also be created by avoiding accentuation in the accompaniment. Overall it may be helpful to try to recreate the sounds and colours of orchestral instruments, with different families of instruments imagined for each layer in the texture.

C:8 Brahms Intermezzo in B flat minor

The introspection of Brahms's late piano works, among which the Three Intermezzos, Op. 117, hold a special place, provides a window into the soul of one of the Romantic era's musical giants. The quasi-improvised nature of the Intermezzo in B flat minor, Op. 117/2, belies the taut control of form and melodic transformation that is a hallmark of Brahms's music. The second main theme (from the upbeat into bar 23) is derived from the opening melody, but almost beyond recognition. The impassioned return of this in the Più adagio that concludes the piece seems to extinguish the warm glow of its first appearance – perhaps a reflection of Brahms's sense of personal loss?

Instrumental intermezzos tend to be lyrical, and allowing the melody to sing in this piece is an important priority. The notes appear dense on the page, so care must be taken to distinguish which belong to the melody itself. Brahms helps in the opening by adding two-note slurs to identify the main tune; at the start, therefore, these are the slurred D♭ to C and subsequent C to B♭, while the other demisemiquavers belong to the accompaniment. The general instruction *col Ped.* encourages pianists to use their discretion in adding to the occasional specified pedalling; the rapid irregular harmonic movement does not always follow the standard beats of the bar, so very attentive listening is advisable.

A successful performance will achieve rhythmic cohesion, and the places where the downbeat is obscured by cross-rhythms, such as with the appearance of the second theme from bar 23, should be noted. Between bar 39 and bar 51 the pulse can become elusive, and a successful performance is one that manages this aural illusion with controlled finesse. The piece builds to a passionate climax at bar 69. The final section can be played considerably slower than the rest, intensely reflective, and the ending cannot feel rushed.

C:9 **Chaminade** Scarf Dance

The prolific French composer Cécile Chaminade (1857–1944) is best remembered today for her many salon pieces, though she also composed a choral symphony and other large-scale compositions. 'Scarf Dance', Op. 37 No. 3, has long been one of Chaminade's better-known compositions – indeed it sold over five million copies during her lifetime – and it shows her talent for exquisite pianism along with melodic and colouristic charm.

It may be useful to lift rather than press down for the quaver figurations, while doing the exact opposite for the chords and octaves. Using arm weight and relaxed wrists with a prepared 'touch and press' approach (fingers placed over the notes in advance of execution) can lead to greater pianistic comfort, as well as to a more beautiful tone quality at all dynamic levels. Chaminade herself asked for the inner melody line to be projected in bars 33–6 and 65–8. This can be achieved by adding extra weight to the RH thumb as it plays each note in turn. It makes sense to use only the thumb for each of the melody notes in this phrase, ensuring that each note is firmly anchored into position using relaxed arm weight. Students should try to feel that the notes above the thumb are simultaneously played with a lifting sensation. By preparing the fingers over the keys in advance it should be possible to produce sensitive sonorities by literally drawing the fingers out of the keys, towards the body.

Chaminade's detailed performance notes refer to her own orchestration of the piece. She stresses the need to control rhythm with discipline. Indeed, this is essential in order to successfully capture this music's balletic, dancing qualities. Pedalling needs careful management throughout. Beginning practice with no pedal at all may be helpful, then gradually adding in what feels essential, being especially wary of blurring the textures as they become denser with the addition of chords and octaves.

C:10 **Fricker** Toccata

The British-born composer Peter Racine Fricker (1920–90) was greatly influenced by serial techniques and jazz in his piano writing. Toccata is the second study in a collection of 12 published in 1962 as his Op. 38. Today it remains his most popular piano piece, an obsessive essay in linear writing that cleverly weaves together triplet figurations based on minor 2nds and 4ths.

Working in isometric rhythms can certainly help with the note-learning process, lengthening one note from each group of three or four notes in turn. Giving some space in this way on different notes as sections of the piece are repeated will enable players to become familiar with all the accidentals. It may also help to work using short-term memory: taking two, three or four groups of semiquavers at a time, students can look at the score until the groups are memorized, then with eyes closed try to play them back from memory. Immediately forgetting what has just been memorized is not a problem – because simply working in this way can accelerate the learning process. It can also be helpful to work at the quieter passages at a much louder dynamic level, even *ff*, then gradually get softer, while keeping a sense of comfort and control. At *p* or *pp*, there is a danger that the playing becomes too inhibited and tense: it therefore makes sense to work initially at a dynamic level that feels innately easier.

A consistent rhythmic emphasis is needed throughout, avoiding accentuation unless it is requested by the composer. For the first half of the study, the default dynamic is *p*, and if the music is played quietly enough then the extended *f*/*ff* passages in the latter half will be much more energized and exciting. The character throughout will be served well if as little pedal as possible is used.

[C:11] Gershwin Prelude No. 1

George Gershwin (1898–1937) was arguably the greatest melodist since Schubert. His unique stylistic synthesis combines influences from jazz, ragtime and the blues, fusing them within the context of a classical framework and aesthetic. The Three Preludes date from 1934 and were originally subtitled 'New World Music'. Gershwin referred to this first of the three as a 'Spanish Prelude', and its extensive use of syncopated energized rhythms and intervals of a 4th evokes something of the spirit and temperament of guitar music and flamenco.

Technically there are various demands here, not least the need to sustain and project accurately all the accents within a strict pulse. Working from a slow tempo and in small sections at a time will be a sensible way forward. The arpeggiated figurations (e.g. the triplet semiquavers in bars 20 and 29) can be assimilated quickly and accurately if practised in block chords. As the piece proceeds the LH's challenges increase. Large leaps, such as those from bar 32, can be worked on in isolation, with 'jump' practice: for the LH leap in bar 32 students should adopt a spring-like action from the low D, moving quickly onto the chord three octaves up. It should feel as though the execution of the low D and the leap that follows it combine into a single movement. This 'play/leap' approach can be used for all the LH jumps towards the end of the prelude. The closing scale flourish might be tried first in groups of four notes at a time, but always using the correct fingering.

🎨 This Prelude can easily be orchestrated in the student's mind – for instance, the opening two bars can be imagined as being played by a muted trumpet, and the melody from bar 7 would work extremely well on the E♭ clarinet. This is the world of Gershwin's *Rhapsody in Blue*, and the touch adopted for much of the syncopated LH accompaniment needs a percussive brightness.

⌈C:12⌋ **W. Mason** Lullaby, Op. 10   (AE)

American pianist and composer William Mason is regarded by many as the 'father of piano pedagogy' in the US. Born in Boston in 1829, he travelled to Europe aged 20, where he became the first American student of Franz Liszt. Returning to his homeland, he is thought to have been the first to give solo recitals there, and composed around 50 pieces which owe a debt to popular European composers of the day. The Lullaby, Op. 10, particularly recalls Chopin's Berceuse, Op. 57, and delights with its subtle melody and rhythmic flow.

This gentle Lullaby is deceptively difficult to bring off effectively. The LH stretches required by the ostinato at the start introduce the biggest challenge of the piece, which will be felt most acutely by those with smaller hands. The suggested fingering is effective, but particular care must be taken to ensure that simultaneous notes are played properly together, and with well-balanced voicing. Where notes are meant to be apart, for example the chord on the second beat of bar 12, the notes should be spread quickly and preferably ahead of the beat. The pedalling indicated at the start will also benefit from careful attention, and underlines the sophistication of the harmonic writing here.

🎨 The gentle barcarolle rhythm needs to be quick enough to communicate two-time, without sounding rushed or leading to untidiness. Rubato can be employed throughout, particularly leading into cadence points, but without becoming too indulgent. Where the composer specifies *poco rit.* and *a tempo*, however, greater licence is possible. In the second half the composer increasingly writes offbeat sforzandos, accents and tenutos simultaneously; the aim here is perhaps to emphasize the tenuto and play these notes with agogic accents, allowing the recurring E♭ some, but not too much, persistence. Dynamics throughout add to the piece's well-constructed shape, but are never louder than *mp*.

⌈C:13⌋ **Poulenc** Improvisation No. 13 in A minor   (AE)

Poulenc considered his 15 Improvisations, which appeared sporadically over two decades and which he subsequently developed, to be the best of his solo piano compositions. The Improvisations are mostly vignettes of personal friendships; No. 13, from 1958, was dedicated to Madame Auguste Lambiotte, of the distinguished Dutch family to whom Poulenc was close. It is one of the most introspective pieces of the set, characterized by quasi-contrapuntal voicing, dramatic outbursts, and the insouciant harmonic twists and ripe modulations that are such a hallmark of Poulenc's style.

Right away the piece encompasses a wide span of notes, often requiring spread chords, large stretches and jumps, and above all attentive pedalling. Although the composer writes *mettre beaucoup de pédale* (use plenty of pedal), there should be no blurring between harmonies; from relatively few notes, Poulenc employs the sustaining pedal to conjure an expansive sound. Where the LH takes the melodic lead, the passage is marked *m.g. en dehors* (LH – *main gauche* – to the fore) to indicate its prominence. Effective voicing between parts is needed here.

Students should make the most of the many expressive contrasts and colours in this piece. Allegretto commodo suggests an 'easy' momentum, not too fast; the metronome indication ♩ = 96 should be considered the maximum speed, and the best performances are often slower. The improvisatory quality lends itself to the use of rubato throughout, not just where specific indications are noted (e.g. in bars 28–30). Dynamics make an equally vital contribution to the overall shape; consider holding back the volume in the *f* passages (e.g. bar 13) in order to heighten the drama of the *ff* when it appears. There are two particular climaxes – the first from bar 22, the second from bar 36. The fluctuating changes from bar 42 to the end create a sense of wistful reflection as the drama diminishes and the Improvisation winds down to its conclusion.

[C:14] **Pozzoli** Berceuse

Italian pianist, composer and teacher Ettore Pozzoli (1873–1957) wrote a good deal of attractive piano music, including several pieces for younger students. He is highly respected for his pedagogic materials and textbooks on music theory and solfeggio, which are still used widely in Italy. Dedicated affectionately to his niece Maria, the Berceuse is a beautifully sentimental piece, combining the pianistic figurations of Chopin's style with sunny harmonies and a deeply affecting melody line reminiscent of Neapolitan song.

While this piece mostly lies well under the fingers, it requires loose, mobile wrists. RH fingering needs care, but alternating between 4/2 and 5/1 at the start sets up a pattern that works well for similar passages throughout. Filigree passages (such as bars 23 and 27) can be broken into groups for practice; while a shimmering effect is ultimately desirable, trying a variety of dynamic levels can solidify finger patterns while developing control. The LH also requires wrist flexibility and some rotation; playing these figures at a softer dynamic is challenging and will benefit from work in isolation, both with and without pedal. The first bass note in each group needs particular weight, and sensitive use of the pedal, to ensure sufficient overall sonority and harmonic clarity.

The nostalgic aspect to this lovely piece allows for more sentimentality in the interpretation than would perhaps be appropriate elsewhere. Expression marks, especially those relating to tempo, can be somewhat exaggerated, but the momentum should not be allowed to dissipate – the basic underlying pulse remaining consistent to the end. Considerable delicacy of touch is required, especially from bar 28, and this effect is further supported by the introduction of the *una corda* pedal in bar 30. The piece can quickly move towards the climax from the crescendo in bar 33 and into bar 36, reaching an apex with the *f* in bar 43; the ending can then drift away with serenity.

[C:15] Timothy Salter Shimmer

This strikingly characterful bagatelle was specially written by the English composer Timothy Salter (b. 1942) for the ABRSM *Spectrum 5* anthology of piano miniatures. Inspired directly by linocut art, the music is a collage of contrasts. It returns consistently to dancing *leggiero* atonal figurations but also contains static, sensuous chordal asides that provide both mystery and ominous darkness before the music continues its balletic journey.

It is important to feel comfortable with and in control of the light staccato required for the opening bar and its subsequent offshoots. Drawing fingers towards the body when playing these semiquavers can be helpful – and practising with as little hand movement as possible, adopting a 'scratching' finger technique in which the fingers do all the work, should yield success, especially if done methodically in small sections of four notes at a time. Working at the staccato passages legato will also instil a familiarity with the note patterns, and in turn a greater sense of security. And the reverse is true too! Bars 31–2 in the LH could prove challenging, but trying them also with staccato articulation using the above 'scratching' approach will lead to an improved sense of digital control.

With so much detail written on the score, the challenge for performers is to capture as many of the instructions as possible. This will lead to a wide spectrum of colours, through different dynamics and touches – which, if realized, will make the music truly come alive. A variety of different pedalling options present themselves and experimenting with these will give further insights into the music. Some phrases are best tackled with no pedal at all, but other sections (notably bars 24–30) can be considered quasi-impressionistic, and will therefore benefit from generous use of the sustaining pedal, as marked.

[C:16] **Turina** La belle Murcienne
(The Beautiful Girl from Murcia)

 Like his compatriot and friend Manuel de Falla, Joaquin Turina spent some time living and studying in France; he was particularly influenced by Impressionism. His vast output of solo piano music includes treasures that reveal both his affinity for the instrument and his mastery of colour. 'La belle Murcienne' comes from *Femmes d'Espagne* (Spanish Women), Op. 73, a set of five musical portraits published in 1932, following an earlier set of 1917. The piece's two contrasting musical ideas portray different qualities – both exoticism, and a simpler beauty.

Those new to Turina's music may find the finger patterns unusual, as they stray far from conventional classical scale archetypes. Time should be taken to devise effective finger substitutions, allowing the RH to play the passages in 3rds, and any inner parts, smoothly. Though marked Più mosso, the middle section has a more lyrical melody, and it may help to play the upper tune in isolation. LH broken-chord figurations throughout require equally careful thought; slow LH-only work may prove essential. Light pedalling is appropriate, but – despite Impressionist influences – too much pedal is best avoided; the vivid colour that imbues this piece is established through the individual notes rather than sustained harmonics.

Tempo changes are somewhat ambiguous and need handling with care. The opening Allegretto is not to be rushed; the harmonic movement allows for a sense of one beat per bar, but demarking RH quavers will help keep the performance rhythmically taut. The Più mosso change may confuse. Here the ♩ = 104 indication is indeed faster than the preceding ♪ = 126, but the overall flow seems calmer due to the relatively static harmony. If students can avoid letting this section drag they will maximize the impact of the climactic *f* from bar 45. The return of the Allegretto and the final Andantino molto tranquillo similarly need to be navigated effectively to bring cohesion to the overall performance.